Heart Mountain

Life in Wyoming's Concentration Camp

Heart Mountain

Life in Wyoming's Concentration Camp

By Mike Mackey

Copyright 2000 by Mike Mackey
All Rights Reserved

A Western History Publications Book
Western History Publications
P. O. Box 291
Powell, Wyoming 82435

Printed by
Mountain States Lithographing
Casper, Wyoming

Cover design by Tina Fagan

Cover Photos courtesy of the Jack Richard Collection
Buffalo Bill Historical Center
Cody, Wyoming

ISBN 0-9661556-3-7

Table of Contents

Dedication

Over the past eight years, a number of individuals have been instrumental in encouraging and guiding me in my study of Japanese relocation and the Heart Mountain experience. The result has been the guest editorship of two scholarly journals, a three-day symposium, involvement in three film documentaries, and the publication of several books and articles. None of this would have been possible without their help and encouragement. This book is dedicated to those individuals, my teachers.

Roger Daniels

Arthur Hansen

Bill Hosokawa

Mamoru Inouye

Roy Jordan

Phil Roberts

Bacon Sakatani

Steve Thulin

Jack Tono

Acknowledgments

For the past eight years, I have been studying various aspects of Japanese relocation in general, and the Heart Mountain experience in particular. This thin volume is the result of much of that study, and many people have helped me along the way. Prior to beginning my research on Heart Mountain, I discussed the subject with my graduate advisor, Philip Roberts, at the University of Wyoming. I explained to Phil that I wanted to reevaluate the sources used by Douglas Nelson twenty years earlier, add sources unavailable to Nelson at the time of his work, and more importantly, include the recollections of life at Heart Mountain collected from former internees. Phil encouraged me in that pursuit, and the result was the basis for this book. Once receiving Phil's approval, I had to locate an individual who would be able to introduce me to former residents of Heart Mountain. That person was Bacon Sakatani. I want to thank Phil and Bacon for their help and encouragement.

This work would not have been possible without the help of nearly forty former Heart Mountain internees. These individuals, whose names are listed in alphabetical order in the bibliography, were willing to share the experiences of a most traumatic time in their lives with a total stranger. I thank them for their confidence and willingness to participate in several of my projects. A number of individuals read the original masters thesis and portions of this manuscript, and variations of it, over the years and made many helpful suggestions. Since this work is directed primarily toward the student and general-interest reader, as opposed to the scholar, I did not always heed or follow through on every suggestion, but this work is greatly improved as a result of comments and critiques from Arthur Hansen, Philip Roberts, Colin Calloway, Lane Hirabayashi and Roger Daniels, for which I am thankful.

During the early research phase of the project Rick Ewig at the University of Wyoming's American Heritage Center was very helpful. Eric Bittner at the National Archives in Denver, Colorado, furnished me with copies of transcripts of several important court cases. Jack Tono shared letters he had located in the FBI files at the National Archives in Washington, D. C. All of those who participated in my *Journal of the West* and *Remembering Heart Mountain* projects contributed greatly to this book (Louis Fiset, Mamoru Inouye, Arthur Hansen, Roger Daniels, Philip Roberts, Frank Van Nuys, Gwenn Jensen, Don Estes, Velma Kessel, Bill Hosokawa, (the late) Frank T. Inouye, and Steve Thulin).

A number of individuals were directly involved with the production of this book. As usual, Winifred Wasden suffered through my writing, taking on the job of copy editing. Tina Fagan handled the cover design, while my wife, Laurie Mackey, assisted with the indexing. Kay Carlson proofread the manuscript and helped me locate photographs in the "Heart Mountain Collection" at Northwest College in Powell, Wyoming. Bacon Sakatani was very generous in allowing me to use photos from his large personal collection. Yo Hosozawa and Toshiko Ito also loaned photographs from their personal collections. Elizabeth Holmes allowed me to use pictures from the Jack Richard Collection at the Buffalo Bill Historical Center in Cody, Wyoming. I want to extend a sincere "Thank You" to these individuals and all of those who helped on this project.

Though many people were involved in seeing this work through to its conclusion, I accept sole responsibility for any errors which may appear in any aspect of the book. I also want to apologize to those individuals who contributed to this project and I have forgotten to acknowledge.

Preface

This thin volume is not a definitive history of the Heart Mountain Relocation Center. That project lies in the future. This book is an attempt to explain certain episodes in the history of the camp and to include the recollections of former Heart Mountain internees who lived that experience. This is, for the most part, their story. Though I hope that this work will be of use to scholars studying the relocation experience, the book was written primarily for the student and general-interest reader concerned with learning more about life at Heart Mountain.

An explanation of terminology will help clarify the work. First, the term, concentration camp, used in reference to Japanese relocation centers, at times infuriates readers who associate the term with Hitler's death camps. There is no comparison between the two. However, concentration camps are what these centers were. The term was used by newspapers and political leaders of the time, including President Roosevelt, to describe the camps. And the idea for the camps was copied from Great Britain's concentration camps which housed South Africans of Dutch ancestry during the Boer War. It seems that those who object most to the use of the term, concentration camp, are individuals who are still trying to justify the "ethnic cleansing" of the West Coast during World War II, and those who never lived within the barbed wire confines of one of these camps.

Throughout the book, the reader will notice that the terms "evacuee," "internee," and "resident," are used interchangeably when describing Japanese Americans interned at Heart Mountain and other camps. "Evacuee" was the term the government preferred when describing Japanese Americans removed from the West Coast. Although Heart Mountain and other relocation centers were not, technically, internment camps, "internee" is the term often used by the Japanese Americans themselves who resided in such centers. They were placed there against their will, had their movements restricted, and were kept under the watchful eye of military guards. The term "resident" is self explanatory.

Some individuals who have read Douglas Nelson's history of Heart Mountain will recognize subjects covered by Nelson but revisited in this volume. The subjects of the draft resisters, efforts of Powell and Cody politicians to exclude the Japanese, and attacks on the camp from the outside are the most notable. I have reevaluated sources used by Nelson and included the recollections of former internees and sources unavailable to Nelson at the time of his work on these topics.

The reader may find discussion of certain aspects of a topic redundant or at times contradictory. I have tried to make this work clear, but this is difficult at times since the entire relocation process was fraught with contradiction. For example, people of Japanese ancestry were removed from the West Coast because they were, according to the government, a threat to the military security of that area. However, in Hawaii, which had been attacked by Imperial Japanese forces, people of Japanese ancestry were not removed. They were described by General Emmons as vital to both military and economic concerns. Also, throughout the war, Japanese Americans who were placed in these camps against their will were continually reminded by both civilian and military officials of their obligations as American citizens. These contradictions were apparently lost on the vast majority of Americans.

As to some incidents seeming redundant, one often runs into repetition when dealing with a large group of people subject to the same experience. In spite of this, I hope that the reader will notice the different effects on individual internees that this shared experience had. This was not a gathering together of like minded people with the same ancestry. If one looks closely when viewing how individual evacuees dealt with their internment experiences, he or she will see a cross-section of America. However, some points or experiences are repetitive. But they are included and repeated because it is my feeling that certain aspects of the relocation experience cannot be over emphasized.

Introduction

On December 7, 1941, the Empire of Japan attacked American military installations in the Hawaiian Islands. This aggression brought the United States into World War II. The attacks carried out by Japanese forces on that date also became a long-sought-after excuse to remove Japanese and Japanese Americans from the West Coast. People of Japanese ancestry were to be moved inland to facilities like the Heart Mountain Relocation Center in Wyoming, due to what some military and civilian leaders described as "military necessity." The bombing of Pearl Harbor alone was the pretext and not the fundamental reason for Japanese relocation. That policy decision was rooted in nearly ninety years of racial prejudice extending back to the days of the California Gold Rush of 1849.

The first large immigration of people of Asian ancestry started when "sojourners" from China began to arrive in California following the discovery of gold at Sutter's Mill. The sojourner hoped to work hard, get rich, and return to his native China. The Chinese referred to California as Gam Saan, meaning "Gold Mountain." It was there that the sojourner hoped to make his fortune. But Chinese immigrants were soon disillusioned. Californians wasted little time in passing laws forcing Chinese immigrants to pay a "foreign miner's tax." However, the Chinese were quickly added to a list of people, which included Blacks and Indians, who could not testify in court against a white person in California. [1]

In spite of these discriminatory actions, the Chinese continued to emigrate to California and other areas in the American West. Although unwelcome in the gold fields, the sojourner could still make more money in America working as a laborer than in his homeland. The Chinese moved into ghettos (ethnic enclaves), most notably in San Francisco, and went into business catering to the needs of their fellow immigrants. A large number worked in the agricultural industry while thousands were employed by railroad contractors throughout the American West. [2]

As time passed, the gold fields played out and the boom in railroad construction ended. The Chinese, who had taken jobs which most whites did not want and who were willing to work for approximately one-half of the wages as white men for the same job, became competitors with America's white laboring class. Although viewed primarily as a problem in the West, by 1870 some Eastern businessmen had used the Chinese as strike breakers. Soon laborers and labor organizations in the East were supporting their brothers out West and calling for an end to Chinese immigration. In 1882 Congress passed the Chinese Exclusion Act, which President Chester A. Arthur signed into law. The law ended the immigration of Chinese laborers for ten years. That law, extended once in 1892, was made permanent in 1902. [3] During that interval, many Chinese returned to their homeland, thus creating a labor shortage in some fields, particularly California's agricultural industry. Japanese immigrants would fill the void created by the departing Chinese.

As the Chinese emigrated to the United States in the 1850s, Japan was still a closed society. Trade with foreign countries and the emigration of its citizens had not been allowed for nearly two centuries. In March 1854, a squadron of American ships commanded by Oliver Hazard Perry sailed into Tokyo Bay. Following negotiations, Japan opened the harbor at Nagasaki to American ships for refueling purposes. Still, Japan remained largely closed, until the restoration of the Meiji Emperor in 1868. In that year, 149 Japanese migrants were allowed to leave Japan to work in the sugar cane fields of Hawaii. With the enactment of the Exclusion Act in 1882, the demand for Japanese laborers increased dramatically. Between 1885 and 1894 nearly 30,000 Japanese laborers emigrated to Hawaii.[4]

Notwithstanding the large numbers of Japanese laborers who emigrated to Hawaii between 1885 and 1894, the Japanese population on the American mainland remained low (approximately 2,500 in 1890, with the majority residing in California). Most were students. Because they required money for living expenses some began working during the summer of 1888 as agricultural field hands. From 1891 to 1900, more than 27,000 Japanese stepped ashore on the United States mainland. Then, between 1901 and 1907, an additional 42,000 Japanese entered the country, most via the Hawaiian Islands.[5]

The larger number of Japanese entering the United States after the turn of the century became a point of concern for California farmers, and later, leaders of organized labor in the American West. The Japanese were compared to the Chinese who had entered the country in large numbers forty years earlier. In May 1905, representatives from a number of organizations in San Francisco met and organized the Asiatic Exclusion League.[6] For the next forty years, the Japanese faced an organized attempt to halt immigration from Japan and, in some cases, to banish Japanese already residing in California.

In October 1906, the San Francisco Board of Education, under pressure from the Asiatic Exclusion League, ordered all students of Japanese or Korean ancestry to be removed from the regular public school system and transferred to the Oriental school then attended by Chinese students. The Board cared little that a number of the Japanese students were "Nisei," the second generation who had been born in the United States and thus were citizens. The difference between the "Issei," the first-generation immigrants from Japan, and their Nisei children, would become crucial to future anti-Japanese legislation imposed by several Western states. According to naturalization statutes passed by Congress in 1790, American citizenship was only available to "free white persons" who immigrated into the United States. The Thirteenth and Fourteenth Amendments to the Constitution granted citizenship to Blacks and all persons born in the United States. However, this still excluded the Issei.[7]

Although the move to exclude students of Japanese ancestry from the regular public school system drew little attention in the United States outside of California, it did make the Tokyo newspapers. The exclusion policy grew into an international incident as the country of Japan, an emerging world power,

ii

envisioned this policy as a loss of face to all Japanese people. Over and beyond the San Francisco School Board action, several bills dealing with anti-Japanese legislation were introduced at that time into both houses of the California State Legislature. To appease both California residents and the Japanese government, President Theodore Roosevelt and Secretary of State Elihu Root worked out the details of "The Gentleman's Agreement."[8]

Under terms of The Gentleman's Agreement, President Roosevelt would, through Executive Order, restrict the immigration of Japanese people from Hawaii, Mexico, and Canada. The Japanese government agreed to stop the emigration of laborers from that country to the United States, but not the wives and children of those already in residence. In return, the San Francisco School Board canceled, for the most part, its exclusion policy aimed at students of Japanese ancestry, and the California Legislature agreed not to enact any discriminatory laws aimed at Japanese people in California. In effect the Japanese government saved face, and exclusionists in California were momentarily placated.[9]

The Japanese understood the agriculture industry quite well, and were not content to work as laborers for white farmers indefinitely. Furthermore, the Japanese were better educated than most immigrant groups and organized quickly, going into business for themselves. By 1904, the Issei owned 4,422 acres of land in California and leased or share-cropped an additional 54,831 acres. By 1909, those numbers had risen to 16,449 acres owned and 139,233 acres leased or share-cropped. The Japanese who continued to labor for other farmers organized to demand parity with workers of European decent. In 1903, nearly 1,000 Japanese and Mexican sugar beet workers went on strike in Oxnard, California, demanding better pay.[10]

The increased amount of land being purchased and leased by the Japanese was only one contributing factor that kept exclusionists in California hard at work. Another factor, which groups like the Asiatic Exclusion League saw as a major problem, was the recently approved Gentleman's Agreement. Due to its familial loophole, between 1908 and 1924, thousands of Japanese women, and some children, emigrated to the United States, primarily to California. Many of those immigrants were "picture brides," women married by proxy in Japan to men in America whom they had never met. Once in the United States, they settled with their husbands and started families. The offspring of these unions were, of course, American citizens.[11] Seeing the Gentleman's Agreement as a sell-out by the federal government, California exclusionists moved to stop what they deemed a Japanese invasion of their state.

By 1913, the California Legislature took action to curtail the ability of the Issei to acquire long-term land leases and own land in their state. The California Alien Land Law passed overwhelmingly in both legislative houses and was signed into law by Governor Hiram Johnson on May 19, 1913. Exclusionists believed that they could stem the tide of immigration and possibly force some Japanese in California to leave the state if they were barred from owning land or acquiring long-term leases. Though land leases were restricted to a maximum of three years, and land purchases by aliens, at least in theory, were ended, the Japanese easily sidestepped the new law. Issei continued to purchase land by putting the title in the name of their American-born children. Also, they circumvented the law by organizing corporations in which their Nisei children or a white attorney were majority stockholders. [12]

Nagamori family in front of their home in Hollywood, California, 1929. The property was owned by the little girl, Toshiko, because her parents were Issei. Photo courtesy of the James and Toshiko Ito collection, hereafter cited as (JTIC).

Following the passage of the Alien Land Law, exclusionists could see that for their program to work as intended, the loopholes in the measure would have to be plugged. Help in addressing the "Japanese problem" in California came in the form of that state's ineffective United States Senator, James D. Phelan. Phelan, a long-time supporter of the anti-Asiatic movement in California, had accomplished little in Washington during his first term. During his bid for re-election in 1920, Phelan's motto was, "Keep California White." Phelan's rhetoric, in combination with revived efforts by groups like the American Legion, Native Sons of the Golden West, and the State Federation of Labor made Japanese exclusion a central theme in the 1919 election. [13]

As a result of petition drives by the Native Sons, American Legion and an assortment of agriculture and labor organizations, an initiative measure was added to the 1920 ballot in California that aimed at excluding the Japanese from owning or leasing farm land. The initiative passed by a vote of 668,483 to 222,086. The provisions of the new law were aimed at denying the Issei access to farm land altogether. The statute stated that the Issei could not pass land onto their American-born children and could not be stockholders in a corporation the like of which the Japanese had used to by-pass the 1913 Alien Land Law. However, once again, the Issei were able to circumvent the new law. The California Supreme Court stated in a 1922 case, Estate of Tesubumi Yano, that the 1920 law could not prevent the Issei from passing land on to their children. As far as leases were concerned, the Issei farmed land that was leased by friendly Caucasians. [14]

It became increasingly clear to California's exclusionists that the 1913 and 1920 Alien Land Laws were ineffective, and that, if they were to exclude the Japanese and halt the immigration of picture brides, action at the national level was needed. Ultimately the passage of the 1924 Immigration Act, though focused primarily on Southern and Eastern Europeans, effectively ended Japanese immigration to the United States. Each country was assigned a quota stating how many of its citizens would be allowed to enter the United States. Japan's quota was set at 100 persons per year. But Congress amended the Immigration Act to exclude the immigration of any person "ineligible to citizenship." [15]

The 1924 Immigration Act's discriminatory policies were more than some Japanese in the United States could stomach. Between 1920 and 1940, the population of foreign-born Japanese in the United States decreased from 81,502 to 47,305. Although exclusionists succeeded, somewhat, in driving out a significant number of the despised Japanese, the Nisei population in the United States increased from 29,508 in 1920 to 79,642 in 1940. Their Issei parents encouraged them to acquire an education and use it to move up the economic ladder. In spite of the fact that the Nisei excelled academically, more often than not, they were forced to retreat to the family business or to accept low paying menial labor upon graduation from college. The exclusionists remained largely silent through the late 1920s and 1930s, but prevailing discriminatory employment practices in the larger American community kept Nisei confined to ethnic enclaves. [16]

Following nearly ninety years of anti-Asian agitation in California, and nearly forty years of anti-Japanese legislation and discriminatory employment practices, the stage was set for the "ethnic cleansing" of the West Coast Japanese

American population upon America's entry into World War II.

Seiichiro Nagamori (left) and Mrs. Mukaeda (right) with stringer of trout caught near West Thumb, Yellowstone National Park, 1939. They were returned to Wyoming three years later and interned at Heart Mountain (JTIC).

Chapter I

The World Turned Upside Down

During the early morning hours of December 7, 1941, naval air forces of the Empire of Japan attacked United States military installations in the Hawaiian Islands. Within hours of that attack, 736 Japanese nationals had been rounded up by agents of the Federal Bureau of Investigation (FBI) in Hawaii and the United States, and turned over to the Immigration and Naturalization Service. The following morning, United States Attorney General Francis Biddle, in a Justice Department news release, informed state and local authorities across the country that there were many people of Japanese ancestry in the United States whose loyalty to this country was unquestioned. Therefore those authorities were to take no action against the Japanese without first consulting with the Justice Department. [1]

Most of those arrested were completely unaware that they had been targeted by the FBI. Iwao Matsushita, a Seattle resident of more than twenty years, answered a knock at the front door and was hustled off to jail at that city's immigration station. Tora Miyake, an elderly woman who made ends meet by giving piano lessons and teaching part-time at a Japanese language school, was one of the few women picked up by the FBI. Miyake, like Matsushita and the others, answered a knock at the door and was quickly hauled off to jail. [2]

The arrests of Japanese, German, and Italian nationals were made under a blanket "Presidential Warrant" which resulted from a proclamation signed by Franklin Roosevelt on December 7, immediately following the bombing of Pearl Harbor. Those picked up were chosen by the FBI, during the months prior to the Japanese attack, as individuals who could pose a potential threat to national security. However, arrests were not restricted to enemy aliens. Any individual, including United States citizens, could be jailed. A local United States Attorney had only to contact the Justice Department and explain his suspicions to have a Presidential Warrant issued for the arrest of any individual in his jurisdiction. And, in case of emergency, when no one at the Justice Department could be reached, arrests could be made without the issuance of a warrant. [3]

The use of such warrants, and the suspicions of local authorities and agents of the FBI led to the arrest of a number of American citizens, sometimes with warrants, and sometimes without. In Seattle, Thomas Masuda and Kenji Ito, both prominent attorneys, were arrested and indicted. Ito's crime was that he had given a speech dealing with Japan's policy toward China, while Masuda had taken pictures at an Armistice Day parade. Both men were tried and acquitted. Bill Hosokawa, who would become the founding editor of the *Heart Mountain Sentinel*, worked for the Japanese consulate in 1938 and had written a letter to a

1

local newspaper asking when any warships might be arriving in the Seattle area. Hosokawa was summoned to appear before the grand jury, but was released when it was decided that he could not be indicted for writing a letter.[4]

In Los Angeles, Togo Tanaka, the Nisei editor of the *Rafu Shimpo*, a Japanese community newspaper in that city, was also presented with a Presidential Warrant and arrested. In spite of the fact that Tanaka was an American citizen, the reason for his arrest was never explained to him. Tanaka was never charged with a crime, yet he was confined in jail for eleven days without being allowed to contact his family or attorney. After a prolonged grilling by FBI agents, Tanaka was told, on the eleventh day, to gather up his belongings and go home.[5]

On December 13, the Justice Department announced that it had arrested 2,541 Axis nationals. Of that number, 1002 were Germans, 169 Italian, and 1,370 Japanese. As the arrests and searches continued, further orders were issued by the Justice Department calling on enemy aliens to forfeit radio transmitters, short wave radio receiving sets and certain types of cameras, to the local authorities. By late December, the FBI had seized 1,458 radios, 2,114 cameras, 2,592 guns, and nearly 200,000 rounds of ammunition. The authorities failed to mention that most of the weapons were shotguns and hunting rifles and, that the ammunition had been purchased at local sporting goods stores.[6]

Seizure of the afore-mentioned property by the FBI was not necessary, as aliens and citizens alike were eager to obey the laws and voluntarily turn over such items. In many instances, it was the local authorities who had trouble following the dictates of the Justice Department. In Washington, a local Japanese merchant read the regulations and saw that he was required to turn his short-wave radio over to the authorities. The merchant packaged up the radio and delivered it to a nearby police station. The officer at the desk refused to take the radio, but did ask the merchant if he possessed a camera or gun. When the merchant explained that he did not own a gun or camera, the police officer sent him home with the radio. The merchant read the order again and returned once more to the police station to surrender the radio. However, he was soon chased from the premises by an irate officer who did not want the short-wave radio. Feeling an obligation to follow the dictates of the law, the merchant returned to the police station, under cover of darkness, set the radio by the front door, and ran home.[7]

At the same time Attorney General Francis Biddle was guiding United States Attorneys and FBI agents in the roundup of potential saboteurs, he was also preaching calm. On December 28 he circulated a news release in which he stated,

> No more short-sighted, wasteful or un-American Policy could possibly be adopted at this time than that of barring non-citizens from legitimate private employment. Our country needs the skills and services of every able-bodied and loyal person, citizen or alien, and to deprive it of such services is an economic waste and a stupid error. [And] there shall be

no discrimination in the employment of workers in defense industries because of race, creed, color or national origin.[8]

Unfortunately, cooler heads did not prevail. By the time Biddle issued this statement, the wholesale firing of people of Japanese ancestry had already begun.

Los Angeles Mayor Fletcher Bowron fired thirty-six Japanese American Civil Service employees. In Seattle, the leaders of the PTA pressed the school board to fire twenty-seven Nisei girls who worked as secretaries for the school district. When board members wavered, the girls all resigned in order to avoid problems. Mitsuye Endo and Ruth Hashimoto were both employed by the State of California and were fired because of their Japanese ancestry (Endo's Supreme Court case would later result in the freeing of all Japanese Americans). Arthur Ishigo, a janitor at a Hollywood film studio was fired. Ishigo's wife, Estelle, a Caucasian woman,

Estelle Ishigo, a Caucasian women, chose internment with her husband Arthur, to separation. Photo courtesy of the Bacon Sakatani collection, hereafter cited as (BSC).

was also fired from her job as an art teacher because she had a Japanese last name. [9]

In addition to the mass firing of Japanese and Japanese Americans, a number of employers refused to pay their former employees once they had been dismissed. In addition, some Caucasian individuals refused to pay rent to their landlords of Japanese ancestry. In an effort to pocket the money and cheat their Japanese employees and landlords out of what was rightfully theirs, these individuals cited a seldom used law which made it illegal to trade with the enemy. However, a California fisherman, Kumezo Kawato, filed suit against his former employer. Kawato's employer stated that since Kawato was an enemy alien he had no right to sue in any court in the United States pending the outcome of the war. Though this line was agreed to by the United States District Court in California, it was overturned by the United States Supreme Court. On November 9, 1942, Justice Black delivered the opinion of the Court stating that even though Kawato was an enemy alien, he was still a lawful resident of the United States.

> A lawful residence implies protection, and a capacity to sue and be sued. A contrary doctrine would be repugnant to sound policy, no less than to justice and humanity. . . . the sole objection to giving judgement for an alien enemy goes only so far as it would give aid and comfort to the other side. [10]

In spite of the Kawato decision, many Japanese and Japanese Americans were cheated out of money due them when war broke out.

In addition to the loss of community leaders resulting from the FBI's arrest of Japanese aliens and some Nisei, Japanese communities were hit again when the Treasury Department froze the assets of Japanese Americans and enemy aliens which were held in American banks and the American branches of Japanese banks in the United States. The FBI also began closing a number of Japanese and Japanese American owned businesses located in West Coast communities adding to already existing hardships. Later a number of businesses were reopened, and Japanese American families were eventually allowed to withdraw up to $100 per month from their personal bank accounts. [11]

As Japanese Americans tried to recover from the hectic events following the attack on Pearl Harbor, individuals and special interest groups on the West Coast began calling for the removal of all persons of Japanese ancestry. Though some political leaders had urged calm and support for their Japanese constituents, those attitudes quickly changed. For example, Earl Millikin, the Mayor of Seattle, met with nearly 1,500 Japanese and Japanese American residents of his community only days after the Pearl Harbor attack and assured those in attendance that they had "nothing to fear while he was mayor." However, several weeks later Millikin informed a congressional committee that Japanese Americans were dangerous and could not be trusted. [12]

During that time, West Coast newspapers, particularly those in California, continually ran stories about radio transmissions to Japanese ships off-shore, caps on tomato plants grown by Japanese farmers pointing toward military installations (these were supposedly to guide Japanese aircraft), and individuals of Japanese ancestry (with invasion maps in their possession) being picked up by the authorities. These stories, none of which were true, were supported by some politicians and military officials. After returning from an inspection of Pearl Harbor in mid December, Secretary of the Navy, Frank Knox, stated in a press conference that the attack on military installations in Hawaii was a result of "the most effective fifth column work that's come out of this war . . . ." Knox was lying. He was simply trying to cover up for the unpreparedness of the military commanders in Hawaii, General Walter Short, and Admiral Husband Kimmel, both whom were relieved of command. [13]

On December 11, Lieutenant General John L. DeWitt was appointed to head the newly formed, Western Defense Command. DeWitt, an army bureaucrat, sixty-one years of age, who had never seen combat, was put in charge of defending the West Coast of the United States. Unsure of himself, and determined not to meet the same fate as his contemporaries, Short and Kimmel, DeWitt called for the exclusion of all enemy aliens above the age of fourteen. The army's Provost Marshal General, Major General Allen Gullion, reviewed DeWitt's exclusion recommendation and felt that the army, not the Justice Department, should have control of affairs dealing with enemy aliens. Gullion sent word to DeWitt that the Los Angeles Chamber of Commerce had contacted the Provost Marshal General's office urging that all people of Japanese ancestry, including American citizens, be locked up. [14]

Initially DeWitt opposed the round up of any American citizen. Though he believed that there were saboteurs in the Japanese American populace, DeWitt felt they could be rooted out without interning everyone of Japanese ancestry on the West Coast. Gullion disagreed and sent Major Karl R. Bendetsen to "help" DeWitt in his dealings with the Japanese Americans. Gullion and Bendetsen, individuals whom historian Roger Daniels has described as "paperwork soldiers," had their own agenda and were determined to see it through to a "correct" conclusion. [15]

The problem which faced Gullion, Bendetsen, the Los Angeles Chamber of Commerce, the American Legion, the Native Sons of the Golden West, and politicians like California's United States Senator Hiram Johnson and California Attorney General Earl Warren and others interested in removing all people of Japanese ancestry from the West Coast, was the same as that faced by supporters of the California Alien Land Law in 1920. Regardless of how some military and political officials, along with special interest groups, felt concerning the Japanese, in order to succeed in having the entire population removed from the West Coast, they would require the tacit approval of the nation as a whole, as had been the case with the passage of the 1924 Immigration Act.

With Gullion and Bendetsen keeping the pressure on DeWitt, Senator Hiram Johnson organized the entire West Coast congressional delegation into a single unit which would lobby its view of the "Japanese problem" at the nation's capital. The addition of opinions by some of America's most respected journalists also helped the cause for removal. Edward R. Murrow told a Seattle audience that if their city was bombed by the Japanese, it was likely that some of the pilots carrying out the attack would be wearing University of Washington sweaters. The liberal commentator on American society, Walter Lippmann, a man said to possess "Olympian wisdom," told his readers that enemy agents on the West Coast were in contact with Japanese ships off-shore. [16]

Henry R. Luce, editor and owner of *Time, Fortune,* and *Life* magazines, also did his part for the removal of Japanese Americans from the West Coast. Luce had been pushing President Roosevelt to get involved in the war as early as 1940. He was a major supporter of the program to send surplus United States Navy warships to England. In addition, Luce was born in China to missionary parents and had a place in his heart for the Chinese people. He despised the Japanese for their invasion of China. When the Japanese attacked Pearl Harbor, Luce was determined that the United States must first defeat the enemy within, and supported the removal of people of Japanese ancestry from the West Coast. Luce used the extensive circulation of *Time* and *Life* to project his views to a wide audience. The March 2, 1942 issue of *Life* showed how both the Germans and the Japanese would invade the United States. Six maps showed the planned invasion routes with five of the six plans illustrating how fifth columnists would assist the Axis landings. One drawing depicted a Japanese tank filling up with gasoline at a California service station. [17]

One week later, *Life* ran a follow up story dealing with the pre-dawn shelling of an oil field approximately twelve miles north of Santa Barbara, California carried out by a Japanese submarine. The submarine which surfaced and lobbed a couple of shells at the oil facilities did little damage. Yet *Life* stated that, "In Tokyo, Imperial headquarters crowed: 'The raid proved to be a great military success.'" [18] At about that same time, Congressman Martin Dies of Texas, chairman of the House committee on un-American activities, made public a 285 page report dealing with Japanese plans to invade the United States. The report contained an invasion map (of unknown origin) and explained how people of Japanese ancestry in the United States passed on important military information to the Japanese Government by notching postage stamps in a certain manner, cutting matches in a matchbook to specific lengths and underlining certain words, using invisible ink, in George Bernard Shaw's, *The Devil's Disciple.* [19]

There were those who opposed any action against Japanese Americans but they were mostly silent. Those who did speak out were largely ignored. Carey McWilliams, one of the most vociferous supporters of Japanese Americans and civil liberties, wrote a number of essays and articles in their support. McWilliams said, "People are prone to forget, in a moment of excitement, that special-interest groups have axes to grind against the Japanese." [20] Louis Fischer pointed out, correctly, that

> the reactionary press and the politicians are out for blood and wholesale internment. Jingoes are endeavoring, under cover of war-time flag-waving patriotism, to do what they always wanted to do in peace time: get rid of the Japanese. . . . liberals, though numerous, are neither vocal nor organized. It hurts them to see clowns in Congress and in editorial offices behave as though they could win the war by attacking Mrs. Roosevelt and sending Japanese children out to Colorado. . . . [21]

Richard Lee Strout attacked Congressman Dies and his committee on un-American activities pointing out that Dies had little understanding of civil liberties. According to Dies, the federal government was too complacent toward the Japanese in California. This was evident to the congressman by the fact that Shinto temples were still allowed to remain open in that state. This comment, according to Strout, only proved that Dies "deplored freedom of religion." [22]

The comments and writings of journalists like Fischer, Strout and McWilliams, were largely ignored. Common sense and civil liberties were not factors considered by the majority of Americans and certainly not by those who possessed ulterior motives as far as the Japanese were concerned. The attitude of those calling for the removal of Japanese and Japanese Americans from the West Coast can best be summed up in a statement made by Assistant Secretary of War John J. McCloy who said, "if it is a question of the safety of the country [and] the Constitution . . . Why the Constitution is just a scrap of paper to me." [23] The problem with McCloy's comment was that the United States mainland was not in danger of attack from the Empire of Japan, and particularly not by Japanese Americans from within.

As the common-sense comments of those who remained calm were ignored, special interest groups and politicians continued to lobby government officials and the military for removal of the Japanese. California's Attorney General, Earl Warren, using a logic that predated Joseph Heller's, *Catch 22*, stated that,

> If we think that sabotage has not been planned for us, we are living in a fool's paradise. The most menacing proof of a real plan is the fact that we have had no sabotage yet. . . . We have been lulled into a false sense of security. Few people realize we are approaching an invasion deadline. [24]

Columnist Carey McWilliams explained Warren's comments when he pointed out that "with 1942 an election year for federal and state officers, some local politicians have suddenly remembered the Yellow Peril, a sure fire political issue in the state." [25] Warren would soon be running for Governor of California.

By early February, 1942, United States Attorney General Francis Biddle was the only hold-out in Roosevelt's cabinet who still opposed the roundup of American citizens of Japanese ancestry. Those who supported the removal of the Japanese realized that to see their plans through they would have to by-pass Biddle and the Justice Department. Major Bendetsen used the comments and concerns of West Coast politicians and special interests to keep the pressure on General DeWitt. If the removal of aliens and citizens was considered to be a "military necessity," Attorney General Biddle could be ignored. [26] By mid February Bendetsen's lobbying efforts reached fruition.

In spite of Biddle's opposition to the roundup of citizens and a report filed by General Mark Clark opposing any "mass exodus" from the West Coast, the politicians, special interest groups and a handful of "paperwork soldiers," succeeded in convincing President Roosevelt and other high-ranking decision makers that an evacuation of Japanese and Japanese Americans might be required as a result of "military necessity." On February 19, 1942, President Franklin Roosevelt signed Executive Order 9066. The Order, which was supposed to help protect the country against espionage and sabotage, directed the Secretary of War to designate military commanders to establish military areas "from which any or all persons may be excluded. . . ." [27] Though Order 9066 does not mention any specific ethnic or racial group, it was designed to deal specifically with Japanese and Japanese Americans.

Within two days of the signing of Executive Order 9066, a congressional committee, headed by California Congressman John H. Tolan, began holding a series of hearings in cities along the West Coast. Nisei leaders met with the committee and brought along Caucasian friends, university professors, and business associates to put in a good word for them. But also testifying were representatives of some special interest groups and area politicians. Among them was Earl Warren, who continued his attack on the Japanese. Warren stated that "there is more potential danger among the group of Japanese who are born in this country than from the alien Japanese who were born in Japan." [28] Bill Hosokawa, who attended the Tolan committee meetings in Seattle, said that the "hearings turned out to be a public forum for 'Jap'-haters . . . ." [29]

With the signing of Executive Order 9066 and the report of the Tolan Committee, the stage had been set for the forced removal of the Japanese, alien and citizen alike, from the West Coast. Though there had been some talk of moving the Japanese "inland," by late February specific sites had yet to be chosen, and the Japanese population was, for the most part, still free.

Chapter II

Attitudes and Rumors in Wyoming

The hysteria concerning the Japanese on the West Coast spread quickly inland. On December 12, five days after the attack on Pearl Harbor, Wyoming Governor Nels Smith sent a letter to all county sheriffs' offices throughout the state. Smith requested that each sheriff's department make a list of all Japanese aliens residing in their counties. The lists were then to be forwarded to the governor's office and turned over to the FBI Regional Office in Denver. [1]

The governor's request was quickly carried out, but it resulted in excessive paperwork for his office and local sheriffs' departments. Smith had so influenced local authorities that they were afraid to let Japanese aliens living within their jurisdiction travel outside the county without permission from the governor himself. Park County Sheriff Frank Blackburn took the governor's orders seriously, but had some reservations as to the necessity of keeping such close tabs on all Japanese aliens residing in Park County.

On January 31, 1942, Sheriff Blackburn wrote to the governor's office asking permission to issue travel permits to a number of the area's Japanese residents. Blackburn explained that most of the Japanese aliens in Park County were farmers living around Powell. Tokuzo Tanikawa and Yozo Tanaka needed to travel to Billings, Montana, in order to purchase seed for spring planting, and they wished to return through Bear Creek, Montana to pick up a load of coal. An area couple, Muragi and Miyono Ando, also wished to make a trip to Billings to visit a daughter. Blackburn said the Andos' five children were American citizens and that he had known all the area farmers of Japanese ancestry for ten to fifteen years. According to the sheriff, they were "all good reliable people" and he asked if it would be possible to issue them permits using his own judgement. [2] It appears as if Smith approved Blackburn's request, though a written response from the governor's office could not be located.

The problems of Japanese and Japanese American residents of Wyoming were the least of Governor Smith's concerns. Rumors were circulating that a number of Japanese aliens were to be sent to Wyoming for the duration of the war. On February 21, Smith wrote to the War Department and the United States Attorney General's office regarding the rumors. The governor said that he should be notified of any such relocation plans and that while Wyoming was willing to do its part for the war effort, the state could not "acquiesce to the importation of these Japanese . . . . " [3] Smith added that if the Japanese were brought into the state they had to be kept under strict federal control and removed from Wyoming at the conclusion of the current emergency. [4]

Smith received support from local politicians and labor organizations in the days after he had contacted officials in Washington. Mayor Ora Bever of Powell told the governor, "We appreciate and agree with you [sic] stand on alien Japs being sent into this state."[5] The United Mine Workers, Local 2309 in Rock Springs, adopted a resolution against accepting Japanese or any aliens from other states. Walter Matson, Local 2309's secretary, said the Japanese people were a danger to Wyoming's railroad and coal industries and he hoped the state could be kept "clean of these people."[6] The *Wyoming Labor Journal* voiced similar concerns: "If the Japanese are dangerous in California they would be in Wyoming. . . . why take chances in wartime with them? American labor does not want to work with them, the way things are now."[7]

In late February, Wyoming newspapers began to run articles concerning rumors of the West Coast evacuation of Japanese into the state. The first rumors, and they were described as rumors, had to do with the use of at least six CCC (Civilian Conservation Corps) camps in Wyoming as possible housing for Japanese aliens. Bizarre stories concerning the Japanese were not limited to West Coast newspapers. A Cody man reported seeing approximately 400 blindfolded Japanese men being marched up the north fork of the Shoshone River.[8]

Not everyone, however, was opposed to bringing aliens into the state. A number of residents had already begun to think of the possible benefits which might boost Wyoming's ailing economy. The majority of the country had been in an economic depression since the Stock Market crash in the autumn of 1929. However, the depression in Wyoming began in 1920 with the conclusion of World War I. Wyoming depended largely on the agriculture and minerals industries. Over production during the war resulted in sharply lower prices for agricultural products following the conclusion of hostilities. In the same light, oil prices in Wyoming plummeted from $3.04 per barrel in 1920 to $1.67 in 1922 and dropped as low as thirty-five cents per barrel in the mid 1930s.[9] The state's coal mining industry was in a similar predicament.

R. T. Baird, editor of the *Powell Tribune,* was enthusiastic about bringing any type of war-related industry to the state. Baird said that Wyoming should do its part for the war effort even if it meant housing "Japs," Germans or Italians. He pointed out that though there was some opposition to this, and while all farmers were not very enthusiastic about the idea, the aliens could be used to help alleviate the existing farm labor shortage.[10]

Governor Smith's stand on the issue was not only popular with some "prominent" people within the state; it also won him letters of approval from individuals in other states. Kenneth Kellar, an attorney from Lead, South Dakota wrote to the governor expressing his feelings on the subject. Kellar said the problem should be handled in a "coldblooded [sic] and ruthless fashion."[11] He explained that everyone knew what a threat the large Japanese population posed to defense industries on the West Coast and he did not think "that any different treatment should be accorded Japanese born American citizens. They shouldn't have been permitted to become citizens in the first place." [12] Kellar added that Japanese women and children should be sent to "concentration areas" and treated properly. However, he felt that all males of Japanese ancestry should be put to work on the construction of the Canada and Alaska highway at the point of a bayonet if necessary. Governor Smith thanked Kellar for the letter and added, "you like the Japs about as well as I do." [13]

E. L. Bennett of Lander, Wyoming also agreed with Smith's point of view concerning the Japanese, but for different reasons. Bennett said there were undoubtedly a large number of loyal Americans among the Japanese but that "most of us are unable to distinguish between Japs, Chinese and Filipinos with any degree of certainty so we are definitely unqualified to tell Jap sheep from Jap goats." [14]

In later months the governor even received a letter of warning and concern from a Mr. Smith in Glendale, California. Mr. Smith told the governor that, "Your state is ideally located to take care of these brown fellows . . . [and] You will be pretty sick of them before you are rid of them. California is." [15] Mr. Smith believed that the government asked California to "soft pedal the Jap issue . . . because they were such wonderful little pagans . . . ." [16] Smith asked the governor why they could not have "Japan for the Japs, [and] America for Americans." He added that the Japanese were "unreliable and tricky and as the record shows only barbarians." [17]

With the February 19 signing of Executive Order 9066, it became more apparent that evacuation might indeed become a reality. While a very vocal minority was presenting its views in support of Governor Smith, larger groups who opposed the removal of Japanese and Japanese Americans from the West Coast were also making their feelings known to Wyoming politicians. The Associated Students of the University of California at Berkeley told Smith that they were very concerned with the future and fate of their Japanese friends. They also said, "we feel that many of those involved are as hard-working, intelligent, loyal, and really American as any student on campus. We hope that you will esteem them as we do, . . ." [18]

After evacuation began Smith was also contacted by the American Baptist Foreign Mission Society. That group, made up of 1,500,000 members, informed the governor that they were very upset by the evacuation of Japanese and Japanese Americans who they believed were loyal to the United States. What bothered the group most was that all actions had been taken against these people solely on the basis of their Japanese ancestry. Charles Inglehart, writing for *The Nation*, agreed, stating, "Discrimination against citizens because of their racial lineage cuts straight across the American tradition." [19]

Throughout March and April, business interests continued to voice their opinions concerning the possible removal of Japanese and Japanese Americans from the West Coast to Wyoming and their possible use as a source of labor.

Alex B. Maycock, vice-president of the Stockmen's Bank in Gillette, Wyoming, informed Governor Smith that there was no need of "Jap" help in his county and said the people did not want them in the county's CCC camp. He also informed the governor that any Wyoming politician who supported allowing the Japanese into the state would have a hard time getting reelected. [20]

W. J. Gorst, of Worland, Wyoming, was president of the Montana-Wyoming Beet Growers Association. Gorst told Smith that his organization was opposed to bringing Japanese people into the area as farm laborers or anything else. There was much more to this issue than sugar beet production. His group would much rather see the U. S. Government bring Mexican Nationals into the country during beet season instead of the "Japs." [21]

While one group of beet farmers opposed bringing people of Japanese ancestry into the state, others saw economic benefits in the idea. A group of Riverton farmers told Governor Smith that due to the draft, high operating costs, and the fact that laborers were leaving the state for higher paying war industries jobs, they would like to see the importation of "native-born Japanese" as a source of labor. The governor informed the group that he would allow Japanese into the state only if they were under the supervision and maintenance of the federal government. [22]

Although the issue of race was often brought up and used as a reason to keep people of Japanese ancestry out of Wyoming, many times the underlying points of contention were economic self interest. The Green River Community Club wanted Governor Smith to allow Japanese evacuees into the state to complete the Seedskadee irrigation project located fifty-five miles north of the town of Green River. On the other hand, the Lincoln County Wool Growers Association opposed the importation of Japanese because they could not be assimilated into Wyoming society. The wool growers believed the Japanese race would push the white race out of the area. In addition, and apparently the real reason for concern, the Seedskadee project would ruin some of the wool growers, prime grazing land. [23]

C. S. Porter, Chairman of the United States Department of Agriculture's War Board in Crook County, had his own project for the Japanese if they were brought to Wyoming. Porter told Governor Smith that approximately 25,000,000 board feet of lumber was being cut annually in Crook County, and that the waste, which was left on the hillsides, was a potential fire hazard. Porter feared that if a fire broke out in such an area and spread to nearby forests, it would devastate the timber industry in that area. Should any Japanese be brought into the state, Porter wanted to use them as laborers to clean up the potential fire hazard. Porter did ask, however, that if the Japanese were evacuated to Wyoming, "they [could] be placed in open areas where danger of sabotage is eliminated?" [24]

On March 31, 1942, Governor Smith received a letter from Milton S. Eisenhower, the newly appointed director of the War Relocation Authority (WRA). The WRA was established on March 18, 1942 with President Roosevelt's signing of Executive Order 9102. This civilian-run organization was established to house, feed and care for Japanese evacuees. In his letter, Eisenhower invited Smith to attend a meeting of western governors to be held on April 7, in Salt Lake City, Utah. The topic of discussion was to be the possible relocation of Japanese and Japanese Americans to the interior of the United States. [25]

At the April meeting of western governors, Eisenhower, assisted by Colonel Karl Bendetsen, informed the governors that a number of sites were being considered in some of their states for the possible construction of relocation centers for the housing of Japanese evacuees from the West Coast. The majority of governors were upset, to say the least, with what Eisenhower had to say. Governor Herbert Maw of Utah said that from an economic standpoint, there were too many laborers in his state as it was. In addition, Utah farmers, Maw said, "prefer Mexican field labor to Japanese . . . ." [26] Nels Smith, while shaking a clinched fist at Eisenhower, said, "If you bring Japanese into my state, I promise they will be hanging from every tree." [27] Only Governor Ralph Carr of Colorado said that his state would welcome the Japanese. According to Carr, it was "the only patriotic choice open to the state." [28]

Following the meeting in Salt Lake City, Governor Smith was more determined than ever not to allow any Japanese into Wyoming unless they were supervised and maintained by the federal government. Upon his return to Cheyenne, Smith was faced with a type of emigration of Japanese from the West Coast to Wyoming, different from that explained by Eisenhower. In a letter, W. C. Miller, acting Chief of Police in Casper, explained to the governor that a Mr. and Mrs. Harry Tsukishima had visited his office requesting a permit to bring Mrs. Tsukishima's brother and his family to Wyoming. Mrs. Tsukishima's brother was forty-one years old and had lived in the United States for twenty-five years. His wife and the couple's three children were all American citizens. The family received a permit to leave California but wanted to be sure they would be allowed to enter Wyoming. Miller asked the governor if there was any procedure the couple should follow that would enable them to enter and settle in Wyoming. [29]

Smith responded to Miller's letter immediately. The governor seemed to chastise Miller for even bringing up the issue. He inferred that Miller should have been well aware of his position as far as importing Japanese into Wyoming. Smith said he had always been opposed to scattering Japanese throughout the state without federal supervision, maintenance and control, and he was, "still of the opinion that the interests of our state can best be served by keeping these people out of our state." [30] The governor also suggested that the Tsukishima family give serious consideration to the fact that they could draw suspicion upon themselves from other members of the Casper community if they tried to help bring West Coast Japanese into Wyoming. [31]

This was not the only incident of that type. Smith was also contacted by the County Attorney from Thermopolis, Wyoming. The County Attorney, Chester

Ingle, stated that a local "Jap" farmer had been to the sheriff's office to see what was required for him to bring in two "Jap" families from California to Hot Springs County. According to Ingle, the "Jap" farmer said he could provide work for two California families. Ingle told the governor that he was well aware of his stand on this issue but that the governor needed to adopt a consistent and uniform policy. Ingle asked for an explanation of the regulations, if any, concerning this type of situation. [32]

Governor Smith was upset with people of Japanese ancestry who were using their rights as American citizens to travel freely within the United States. He contacted Secretary of War Henry Stimson to voice his concerns. The governor informed Stimson of the promises made by Milton Eisenhower to all western governors who had attended the Salt Lake City meetings. The guarantee was that no Japanese would be brought into any of the states unless they were under federal supervision and maintenance. Smith said he had been informed that three Japanese families had moved to an area near Worland, Wyoming and that these families were not under federal supervision or maintenance. He also added that, "The state of Wyoming is unalterably opposed to permitting Japanese to come within our borders except under federal supervision." [33]

Stimson pointed out that no Japanese were moved into Wyoming by the federal government or the War Department. He said that there were a number of Japanese Americans who did not reside in any of the military zones on the West Coast and those people were free to travel in any of the interior states they chose. Stimson, who was busy trying to deal with America's involvement in a World War, explained to Smith that at that time there were other considerations far more important than three families of Japanese ancestry moving to Worland, Wyoming. [34]

From shortly after the attack on Pearl Harbor through the end of April 1942, Wyoming Governor Nels Smith spent a good deal of time trying to keep people of Japanese ancestry out of the state. Some Wyomingites supported his stand; others saw the potential economic advantages in having some Japanese and Japanese Americans relocated to Wyoming. Smith saw the silence of the majority of Wyoming's citizens on this issue as tacit approval for his stand. By the end of April, and the first week of May, evacuation finally became a reality. People of Japanese ancestry, both aliens and American citizens, were being sent to assembly centers at different locations on the West Coast, and in spite of Governor Smith's comment that if brought to Wyoming the Japanese would "be hanging from every tree," they would soon be moved inland.

Chapter III

Forced Removal and the Assembly Centers

While Wyoming's Governor Nels Smith was doing everything in his power to insure that no Japanese were brought into his state, General John DeWitt was in the process of complicating the governor's life. On March 2, 1942 General DeWitt divided the states of Arizona, California, Oregon and Washington into two military areas. Area No. 1 was then further divided into a prohibited zone, which ran along the Pacific Coast, and a restricted zone. All Japanese and Japanese Americans were, eventually, to be removed from Area No. 1. However, originally there was no plan to remove anyone from Area No. 2, and some Japanese Americans voluntarily relocated there. But in time, the politicians and special interest groups succeeded in also having the Japanese removed from that Area. [1]

Japanese and Japanese Americans were removed from Terminal Island near Los Angeles in February; however, other people of Japanese ancestry were not removed from Area No. 1 until the end of March. The removal of more than 100,000 people from a large geographic area would take practice. This practice run took place near Seattle with the removal of approximately forty-five Japanese families from Bainbridge Island in Puget Sound. The order for the forced evacuation of the Bainbridge Islanders was issued by DeWitt on March 24, 1942. The island's residents were told to be ready to move within a week. [2]

The evacuation at Bainbridge Island was closely monitored by Tom Rathbone, a federal government employee, who watched for any problems that might arise. In a report to Army authorities following the Bainbridge evacuation, Rathbone suggested that a more complete set of instructions for the evacuees would facilitate less troublesome moves in the future. The biggest problem Rathbone observed was the care and disposition of the evacuees' personal property. Several days prior to the relocation process, a rumor began circulating among the Bainbridge Island residents that the government would pay to transport personal property to the relocation sites. Some Japanese who sold their personal possessions for next to nothing began buying them back. The day prior to their removal the Japanese were told that the government would not pay to ship personal items to evacuees once they relocated, nor would it pay to have that property put into storage. Rathbone said the issue of personal property had to be resolved before further evacuations were undertaken. [3]

With the successful and uneventful removal of the Bainbridge Islanders, the rest of the West Coast was divided into 107 evacuation districts. Each district contained approximately 1,000 people of Japanese ancestry. Through April and May 1942, Exclusion Orders were posted throughout each of the 107 districts. The Orders gave Japanese residents one week to ten days to store, or sell, personal

15

possessions prior to reporting to a designated assembly point. From the central gathering point, the evacuees were tagged, numbered, and sent to one of fifteen temporary camps known as "assembly centers." Failure to report by the designated time was a violation of federal law. Public Law 503, passed by both houses of Congress without a single dissenting vote, made it a federal offense to remain in a military area once an individual had been ordered to leave. Senator Robert Taft said that PL 503 was the "sloppiest criminal law he had ever seen, . . ." but he agreed to vote for it since it was directed only toward the Japanese. [4]

During the weeks following the attack on Pearl Harbor when government officials were considering which people should be removed from strategic areas, it was felt that only individuals fourteen years of age and older posed an actual threat as far as sabotage was concerned. However, as evacuation began in earnest, Karl Bendetsen, who was overseeing the operation for the army, was determined to remove everyone of Japanese ancestry from the West Coast. Father Hugh Lavery, caretaker of a Catholic Maryknoll orphanage in Los Angeles, reported to Bendetsen that the orphanage was home to some children of Japanese ancestry, some one-half Japanese, others one-quarter or less. Lavery asked what the policy was as far as the orphans were concerned. Bendetsen told Father Lavery, 'I am determined that if they have one drop of Japanese blood in them, they must go to camp.' [5] Bendetsen's policy resulted in the establishment of The Children's Village, a camp within a camp, located at the Manzanar Relocation Center. The Children's Village was home to 101 Japanese American orphans and was the only orphanage in the relocation camp system. [6]

By early April, the forced removal of the Japanese was in full-swing. On April 2, Frank Duveneck, a resident of Los Altos, arrived in San Francisco with his wife to assist a family he knew in moving from their home to the assembly area on Van Ness Avenue. As Duveneck wandered through the neighborhood he observed notices posted on walls and telephone poles with directions and requirements for the Japanese evacuees to follow. Duveneck said, "My mind went back to similar notices that I saw in Germany some years ago, proclaiming restrictions against the Jews." [7] There were a number of Japanese men wearing American Legion caps. One such individual told Duveneck that he thought serving in the United States Army during World War I entitled him to stay in his home. Duveneck wondered how anyone could "consider the color of a man's skin a test of his loyalty." [8]

As in San Francisco, the evacuations continued up and down the West Coast. Charles Kikuchi was evacuated from Berkeley on April 30. His family had been removed from San Francisco several weeks earlier, but Kikuchi stayed in Berkeley to complete his final exams at the University of California before being evacuated. Prior to moving to the designated assembly point, Kikuchi stopped by the bank to close his account. The bank teller shook his hand and said, "Goodbye, have a nice time." As he walked toward the assembly area Kikuchi said a number of young children in the neighborhood were running up and down the street yelling, "The Japs are leaving, hurrah, hurrah!"[9] The evacuees ignored the children and continued toward their destination.

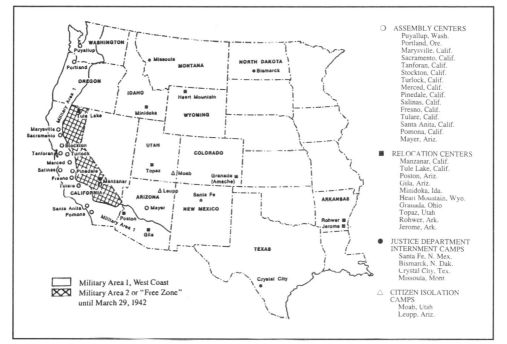

Map indicates the locations of assembly centers and different camps. Map courtesy of John Estes, Department of Geography, University of California, Santa Barbara.

From gathering points in the 107 evacuation areas, the Japanese and Japanese Americans were sent by bus or train to one of fifteen assembly centers located from Arizona to Washington. The assembly centers were constructed, for the most part, at horse racing tracks and fairgrounds. The military felt that these large open areas could be easily guarded. The fairgrounds and race tracks also had water supplies and often exhibition halls, which could be converted to mess facilities. Many of these locations already had some housing available. That "housing" took the form of horse stalls which were quickly whitewashed, often right over the manure which was stuck to the walls. Each horse stall became the residence of one family. During the early weeks of the evacuation, the assembly centers, which had previously housed animals, were ill prepared to handle the new human residents. [10]

Although there were fifteen assembly centers, more than 10,000 of Heart Mountain's internees came from three located at the Santa Anita Racetrack in

Arcadia, California, the Pomona Fairgrounds in Pomona, California, and the Portland, Oregon Livestock Exposition Hall. There were 1,000 people from the Portland center, 5,100 from Pomona and 4,600 from Santa Anita. The Pomona and Santa Anita centers were located in Southern California near Los Angeles. [11]

The initial evacuation resulted not only in the uprooting of families, but also, as mentioned previously, in a great loss of personal possessions. Following the confusion at Bainbridge Island, the government decided that evacuees would be allowed to take only those belongings they could carry. Many possessions were lost or had to be sold for next to nothing. Describing "evacuation sales," Charles Kikuchi said the junk dealers had it made. "They buy cheap from the Japanese leaving and sell dearly to the Okies coming in for defense work." [12] Some families stored their belongings with friends or in the basements of neighborhood churches. In addition to personal items, some Japanese had land and businesses to dispose of or lease to someone who they hoped would care for it in their absence.

Ben Okura's parents owned nine acres of farm land which was still mortgaged. The property, because of California's Alien Land Law which prohibited aliens from owning land, was in the name of one of the Okura's five sons. Nevertheless, the mortgage had to be taken care of before the family was evacuated. The Okuras had one week to "wrap things up and get the hell out." The family did not know where they were going or if they would ever be able to return to California. To this day family members still have deep resentments concerning the forced sale of their land. [13]

The Okura family was sent to the Pomona Assembly Center in May 1942. Ben Okura, a recent high school graduate at the time, remembered being told that the evacuation was for their own protection. He found it strange that guards who were supposed to be protecting his family and other Japanese and Japanese Americans, were escorting him into the fenced enclosure at Pomona and then intently watching the crowd inside. The guards were not concerned with activities outside the center from where the supposed threat to the internees' safety would come. [14]

Pomona was also the destination for Kumezo Hatchimonji, his wife, and three children. Hatchimonji had received a B.A. in business from Columbia University and was an independent businessman when his family was uprooted. Ike Hatchimonji said the family was forced to give away, or sell at giveaway prices, their two cars and many other personal belongings. The few items that they had put into storage were stolen by vandals while the family was interned. [15]

Both Ike and Mike Hatchimonji (14 year old twins), upon arrival at Pomona, said they had never seen so many Japanese people in one place in their lives. Both of the boys had attended schools where the student body was predominantly Caucasian. Ike remembered Pomona as a bleak place. Meals were served in hot crowded mess halls where people waited in line, sometimes up to an hour, to be fed. The jerry-built barracks were very crude. The ceilings were open and there were often gaps up to one-half inch wide between the wall boards. Privacy was unheard of. A common building contained the toilet and shower facilities. Mattresses were cotton muslin bags which each internee filled with straw or hay from the stacks inside the center. Some of the few bright spots Ike remembered were visits from the American Friends Service Committee (the Quakers). They would come in, visit, and then leave gifts such as jigsaw puzzles which helped break up the monotony of life in the center. [16]

Frank Hayami was twenty-two years old and had been attending the University of California at Berkeley when he was marched off to the Pomona Assembly Center. Hayami was living in a horse stall at the Pomona Fairgrounds when the mailman delivered his diploma. He received a degree in electrical engineering from U. C. Berkeley and celebrated his graduation at the center. [17] Many other evacuee college graduates from up and down the West Coast received their diplomas under similar circumstances.

Jean (Miwa) Ushijima was nine years old and living in San Francisco when evacuation began. She said that a doctor checked everyone over before they were sent to the Pomona Assembly Center. Ushijima had a cold and was afraid the doctor would not let her travel with her parents. All that she could remember about Pomona was the heat and boredom. [18]

Yas (Morita) Ikeda was another young girl living in San Francisco. Since the Tanforan Assembly Center was so close by, she thought that her family would be sent there. However, like Jean Ushijima, Ikeda and her family were transported south to Pomona with no explanation. Evacuation seemed to be a hit and miss process as far as where one ended up. Ikeda said that her parents were hastily trying to liquidate their business before being evacuated, but as a young girl, she was not too concerned about what was happening. Most vivid in her memory were heat and the long lines at the Pomona mess halls. The community bathrooms, especially a basin filled with some type of liquid that was supposed to prevent athlete's foot, also left a clear picture in her mind. Everyone was supposed to step into the basin when entering or leaving the shower area. [19]

Joyce Mori, who was also sent to Pomona, described the day her family was evacuated as, "very traumatic." While her parents were trying to decide what to take and what to leave behind, Mori and her younger sister were more concerned with being forced to give up their pets. At Pomona, Mori's family of six was placed in one small room. Each member of the family received a cot and a mattress which had to be taken to the nearby straw pile and filled. Leaving a good mattress behind and being forced to sleep on a straw or hay filled mattress was bad enough, but Mori's mother, and several of their neighbors, suffered from severe hay-fever and were in a state of constant misery. [20] Yosh Sogioka, another Pomona resident, said that the smell of straw and hay made him feel like he was living in a manger. [21] Technically speaking, he was.

The assembly centers like Pomona also led to social problems. Although most internees did not mention the breakdown of the family unit until after reaching relocation centers like Heart Mountain, Yosh Sogioka noticed the beginning of that deterioration at Pomona. The father was the strong central figure in the Japanese family. He was the provider and received great respect from all other members of the family. In a mess hall situation, adolescents no longer needed their fathers or the family unit to provide for them. Sogioka said the mess hall was a major factor which led to the eventual breakdown of the family. Destruction of the family unit was only one of a number of byproducts of evacuation. [22]

Tatsu Hori was a graduate of U. C. Berkeley with a degree in engineering. After being turned down for a job by Lockheed, whose representative said during a visit to the university that the company would hire anyone who graduated, Hori worked in New York for a time before returning to the San Francisco Bay Area. Upon his return, he worked designing air conditioning systems. When evacuation came, Hori, who had heard how bad the Tanforan Assembly Center near San Francisco was, requested permission to be relocated to another facility, since his mother was in poor health. The government granted his request and sent Hori and his mother to Pomona. He said that despite the injustice, the restrictions and confinement, the people at Pomona really came together as a community. [23]

Rose (Tsuneishi) Yamashiro and her family lived so close to Santa Anita that they were sure that it would be their destination. But the family was sent to Pomona. Her sister, whose whole life was music, was forced to sell her piano for $25 or $30. The rest of the family's belongings that were not sold were stored in the house in which they had been living. Despite this, many of their possessions were never seen again. Following the war it was found that approximately eighty percent of possessions privately stored by evacuees had been "rifled, stolen or sold during absence." [24]

What Yamashiro remembered most about Pomona was the zoo-like atmosphere with all the activity and confusion. But it was the bed-checks which she found most annoying. When the family was trying to sleep at night, guards or assembly center policemen would come in and shine flashlights in their eyes while taking a head count. The spaces between wall boards and the large knotholes through which one could look into the room of the family next door, and the complete lack of privacy, also stuck in her mind. [25]

Art Tsuneishi and Toyoo Nitake each had one specific memory of the assembly center experience. Tsuneishi recalled the irony of Pomona. Prior to evacuation it had been a special place for the family. His parents had always taken the whole family to the fair at Pomona every year. Now they were incarcerated there. Toyoo Nitake said that it was the first time in his life he had ever seen guard towers and armed guards. Jack Oda remembered his arrival at Pomona as a shock and a rude awakening. He too was dismayed by the fenced enclosure and the armed guards. [26]

In many ways, life at Santa Anita was similar to that experienced at

Pomona. There were, however, some differences. Santa Anita was the largest of the fifteen assembly centers. At its peak it housed nearly 19,000 people. Toshiko (Nagamori) Ito was one of those incarcerated at Santa Anita prior to being sent on to Heart Mountain. The first things she saw at the assembly center were guard towers with searchlights, barbed wire, and armed guards with rifles and bayonets attached. After relating this experience to a church group years later, Ito was told by a woman who had lived near the Santa Anita Race Track during evacuation that she did not remember seeing armed guards or barbed wire. The woman also explained to Mrs. Ito that the latter should have felt fortunate to have been able to live in such a beautiful area as Santa Anita.[27]

Men's latrine at Heart Mountain. Note the lack of privacy. These facilities were somewhat similar to those at the assembly centers. Drawing by Estelle Ishigo (BSC).

Ito said the first to arrive at Santa Anita were housed in stables which had been quickly swept out and white-washed. Neither the white-wash nor the sweeping eliminated the smell of horses. The barracks, constructed to house other evacuees, were built with green lumber, and like Pomona, offered no privacy. When the lumber dried and shrank it left large spaces between the boards. At

Santa Anita, as at Pomona, the first job was to fill one's mattress with straw. The community showers were in the same area where the horses had been washed and groomed. The stench was ever present. The shower jets protruded from the walls, and there were no partitions. In the women's latrine, there were partitions between the toilets but no doors. The last stall on the end was the most popular because it offered some privacy. The toilets in the men's latrine did not even have partitions. A low table and water were provided for washing clothes, but the internees were forced to buy wash tubs, scrub boards and usually child's wagons. The wagons, usually purchased from the Sears or Montgomery Ward mail order catalogue, were used to haul clothing and utensils to the wash-racks. [28] The bathing and toilet facilities were what many people on the outside referred to as "modern conveniences."

Jack Tono's family was sent from San Jose to Santa Anita. The Tonos left everything that they were not allowed to take with them in their home in San Jose. Tono said he knew the house would be burglarized and everything his parents had worked for lost while they were interned. He was right. Tono would never get over being incarcerated simply because he was of Japanese ancestry. He found the others at Santa Anita to be in the same mood as his family. All seemed to be in a state of shock, which in many instances has not been erased, even with the passing of more than fifty years. Tono also remembered the smell of horses that rose out of the asphalt, and the alfalfa that grew in the cracks of the barracks floors. Nearly everyone who wanted to work was given a job at Santa Anita. One of the main projects was constructing camouflage netting for the army. Here was a group of people who had been declared 4-C (enemy aliens)–a "potential threat" to national security–working on defense projects. [29]

Since Ruth Hashimoto was bilingual, she was hired as a secretary and interpreter by the Provost Marshall General's office. For that reason she and her family did not leave for Santa Anita until Memorial Day of 1942. Her most distinct memory of the assembly center was standing in line. With the almost 19,000 people who were at Santa Anita, standing in line was the main occupation of most residents. Hashimoto also remembered the work stoppage and strike by the 800 workers who were constructing the camouflage nets. When the workers learned that those on the outside were being paid more money to make the same nets, they went on strike. The military decided early on that an internee could not be paid more than a private in the army, who at that time would have earned $21 per month. The professionals in the center, doctors, teachers and the like, were the highest paid evacuee workers receiving $19 per month. The unskilled laborers were paid $12 per month and the semi-skilled received $16 per month. The army investigated the situation but could not understand why the workers went on strike. [30]

Mori Shimada was another evacuee who worked making camouflage nets at Santa Anita. Like many of the others, his most lasting memory of the center was the smell of horses and manure that constantly rose up out of the asphalt. Emi Kuromiya was also at Santa Anita. She arrived only two months after her wedding. Kuromiya felt that her family had been lucky since they were allowed to store their personal possessions in the basement of a Methodist Church before being evacuated. Unfortunately, books and family photos were destroyed in a flood while the family was interned. [31]

Grandstand area at the Santa Anita Assembly Center was used by internees for Sunday church services and was where residents hung the camouflaged netting they worked on. Drawing by internee artist, Sakaguchi (JTIC).

Dyaney Ota arrived at Santa Anita under much different circumstances. Ota worked for the Los Angeles County Sheriff's Department until January 1942. Ota, her husband and three-year-old daughter were preparing to leave for Wyoming when they asked local authorities if they first had to meet any requirements. The Otas were told to report to the nearest assembly center for a supposed two-week stay, after which they would be allowed to leave and join 100 other families traveling to the Midwest. Three and one-half months later the Ota's were still incarcerated at Santa Anita. [32]

After more than three months of waiting, Ota wrote to Governor Nels Smith explaining her situation. She told the governor that she was born in Wyoming, and that her parents had lived in Rock Springs for thirty-seven years. Her brother, Frank Ikuno, was employed by the Wyoming Highway Department in Cheyenne. Ota and her husband had already secured jobs in Rock Springs. They were simply seeking permission from the governor to return to the state. [33] There is no record of a response from Governor Smith, and the fate of the Ota family is unknown.

The experiences of Heart Mountain residents sent to the Portland Assembly Center were very similar to those who were removed to Pomona and Santa Anita. Most evacuees stayed in the assembly centers from late April or early May 1942, until August or September 1942, depending on when they were sent to the more permanent relocation camps.

While the people of Japanese ancestry endured life in the assembly centers, the government had given the go-ahead for construction of eight relocation camps located farther inland (two assembly centers in California, Manzanar and Tule Lake, also became permanent facilities). The Heart Mountain relocation center was one such camp. The construction phase of the Heart Mountain camp provided employment for a large number of people in Northwest Wyoming. The work benefitted laborers and merchants in Powell and Cody for two months. But there were others in the area who were looking for more long-term economic benefits from the camp.

Chapter IV

Heart Mountain and Economic Opportunities
in Northwest Wyoming

As Japanese Americans were being rounded up and sent to assembly centers, the decision was made by the WRA to go ahead with the construction of permanent relocation camps. The states of California, Arizona and Arkansas would have two camps each. Colorado, Utah, Idaho and Wyoming would each have one camp constructed within their borders. A number of communities in Wyoming expressed interest in the relocation camp projects. The town of Worland made a concerted effort to bring a relocation center or a prisoner-of-war camp to that area. Worland had a number of projects in the works for which a great deal of cheap manual labor was required. Early in April 1942, Worland Mayor Ray Bower contacted Wyoming Senator Joseph C. O'Mahoney to ask for assistance in acquiring a camp for his town. The senator informed Bower that sentiment in Wyoming concerning evacuee camps was sharply divided, but that he would do what he could. O'Mahoney suggested that the mayor contact Milton Eisenhower of the WRA to find out what steps to follow. [1]

Upon hearing from the senator, Bower called a meeting of the Alfalfa Commercial Club (Worland Chamber of Commerce) to present his proposal. The meeting was also attended by members of the Lions Club and a number of area sugar beet growers. W. J. Gorst, President of the Montana-Wyoming Beet Growers Association, had told Governor Smith a month earlier that his organization did not want any Japanese brought into the area to work the beet fields. Gorst apparently did not consult many of his members before coming to that conclusion. Not only did a number of area growers attend the meeting, but L. E. Laird, plant manager for Holly Sugar Corporation's Worland processing facility, was also in contact with O'Mahoney on behalf of beet growers who were interested in a war-time labor force. [2]

The consensus at the meeting was that Worland should make every effort to get a "Japanese Labor Highway Camp." The labor from such a camp would be used mainly to construct the "Gooseberry Tie-in." The tie-in was a section of highway that would create a shortcut to Yellowstone Park and possibly increase tourism through Worland in the future. Those at the meeting also said such a camp would provide a pool of labor that could be tapped by farmers when it came time for the sugar beet harvest. Bower said that such a camp should be controlled and financed by the federal government. He believed that government control would quell any "objection against a white american [sic] community having to eventually absorb an excess of Japanese." [3]

By early May, Governor Smith, who three weeks earlier said that if

25

Japanese were allowed into his state they would "be hanging from every tree," was contacting the Provost Marshal General's office on behalf of the town of Worland. At that same time, however, Milton Eisenhower of the WRA informed Senator O'Mahoney that the use of CCC camps as relocation centers, which Worland and some other communities proposed, was not practical. Eisenhower said that the WRA had set a minimum population for relocation centers at 5,000. That number was based on calculation as to how many troops would be necessary to "protect" the evacuees. He pointed out that the army was not willing to send troops all over the country with evacuees and that the WRA was looking at a maximum of fifteen to eighteen camps. Eisenhower did not believe that any CCC camps in Wyoming were capable of handling 5,000 people, and said most sites for relocation centers had already been chosen. [4]

During the first week of June, 1942, Senator O'Mahoney contacted the Alfalfa Commercial Club in Worland to inform its members that the WRA had approved only one site in Wyoming for a relocation center. The site, in Northwest Wyoming, was located on the 42,000 acre Heart Mountain Reclamation Project between the towns of Cody and Powell. Upon receiving this news, the Worland group began to pursue the possibility of acquiring a prisoner-of-war camp, again in an effort to exploit a possible labor source for their own benefit. Assistant Secretary of War, John J. McCloy, told Senator O'Mahoney that the government had all the prisoner-of-war camps that it would need for the time being. [5]

While Worland had been lobbying for its own relocation center or prisoner-of-war camp, Senator O'Mahoney was taking a survey in the towns of Powell and Cody. He was trying to get a feeling for the local attitude toward the proposed Heart Mountain Relocation Center. Cody attorney Paul Greever said the establishment of a camp at Heart Mountain would not disturb his peace of mind, but he suggested that there be proper supervision. Mayor Paul Stock of Cody said he would not welcome the Japanese in the community itself, but if they were kept in the camp and properly supervised it would be acceptable. Park County Commissioner Harry Attebery said he found that generally there was opposition to bringing the Japanese into the county. He felt, however, that if the federal government would closely guard these people and remove them from the county after the war, there would be no problems. Attebery said that without proper supervision, the Japanese could be a menace to nearby irrigation projects, "One stick of explosive in the Corbett Tunnel would destroy the water supply for the irrigation of about 60,000 acres . . . ." [6] Don Jamieson of The Powell Club (Powell Chamber of Commerce) informed the senator that his group was very interested in the relocation center, while Jack Richard, editor of the *Cody Enterprise*, had no problem with the establishment of a camp even though he had "no love of the Japanese." [7]

By early June 1942, the Heart Mountain Relocation Center was becoming a reality. The camp was to be built on land which was a part of the Heart Mountain

Federal Reclamation Project halfway between Powell and Cody, Wyoming. It was to be large enough to house at least 10,000 Japanese. According to R. T. Baird, editor of the *Powell Tribune*, the new residents were to, "level the land, put in irrigation ditches, prepare the land for cultivation, . . . [and] they will not be permitted to mingle with outsiders."[8]

Workers constructing barracks at Heart Mountain. Photo by Jack Richard, Bacon Sakatani collection, hereafter cited (JR-BSC).

The effect that this camp would have on the two small Wyoming communities was described by Baird as a "big boon to business–the biggest thing in the way of industrial and payroll activity that has ever come to Powell."[9] Powell and Cody became busy towns as enough workers were hired to complete construction of the camp in sixty days. Advertisements in local newspapers sought housing for the more than 2,000 workers who were expected to come into the area. A number of local workers quit steady jobs in the hope of earning the higher wages paid by the government in connection with the camp's construction.[10]

Within only four weeks of the beginning of construction of the camp, "The payroll from Heart Mountain Relocation Center . . . brought good times and busy times to Powell."[11] The project was described as an answer to prayers that somehow the Big Horn Basin would get a share of the billions of dollars being spent on the war effort. R. T. Baird said that, "The whole thing was like a dream come true."[12]

The influx of construction workers at Heart Mountain brought economic good-times to Powell and Cody (JR-BSC).

With the camp under construction, a number of area businessmen were also looking to profit from the relocation center and the Japanese and Japanese Americans who were to be incarcerated there. Senator O'Mahoney was flooded with requests, from the Big Horn Basin's private sector, for help in obtaining government contracts for businessmen.

George Reesy, the owner of Reesy Drug Store in Thermopolis, told O'Mahoney that he was interested in a drug store concession at the "Jap Camp." Reesy was curious as to whether or not the government was going to be "giving all such concessions, to the Japs . . . "[13] or if any would be given to outsiders. J. A. Morrow of Riverton and Paul Greever of Cody contacted the senator on behalf of George Bonner of Greybull and C. H. Scribner of Riverton. The two men were interested in acquiring a permit which would enable them to open up a store within the confines of the camp. It was to be something "along the line of a junior department, [sic] store, . . ."[14]

Stores or concessions at Heart Mountain were not the only possibility of economic benefit in the Powell and Cody area. Dick Jones, owner of Powell Transfer & Storage Company, was trying to obtain information on how to put in a bid for the transportation of coal to the camp (coal was eventually hauled in by Burlington Northern Railroad Co.). Clyde Gorrell was working through Paul Greever in an effort to be awarded the camp's garbage disposal contract, while Oliver Steadman, secretary of the Cody Club (Cody Chamber of Commerce), was asking Senator O'Mahoney if it were not possible to enlarge the center. The economic situation was so good for the business community in Cody during the construction phase of the relocation camp, that Steadman thought the center should be expanded. [15]

Heart Mountain Relocation Center under construction (JR-BSC).

One of those who received the greatest economic benefit from Heart Mountain after the camp was occupied was T. T. Dodson, owner of the Powell Valley Creamery. Dodson contacted senior administrative official John Nelson at Heart Mountain, and after extensive discussions, came away believing that he had a good chance at obtaining the milk contract for the camp. Dodson, however, would have to increase his base supply of milk in order to fulfill current obligations plus those of the camp. [16]

Dodson received the contract in mid August. The first contract was for thirty days, but after that it was to be renewed every three months. The creamery owner was obligated to deliver 500 gallons of milk four times per week. In order to meet those needs, Dodson called on area dairy farmers to increase the size of their herds and obtained milk from as far away as Bridger, Montana. The Heart Mountain milk contract made the Powell Creamery the third largest in the state of Wyoming. It also contributed an estimated $10,000 per month to the income of area dairy farmers. [17]

Dodson was not content to profit from Heart Mountain while it was in operation and then return to the way things were after the camp closed. In January 1943 he purchased the Rock Creek Cheese Factory in Roberts, Montana and moved it to Powell. Dodson estimated that by the time he put the cheese factory into operation, the camp would be ready to close. [18] He could then use the milk previously sold to Heart Mountain for the production of cheese.

Once the camp was occupied, a number of smaller businesses in Powell and Cody also benefitted directly from the relocation center. Tom Scott, the shoe cobbler in Powell, had a large increase in business, and he expressed his thanks to the "soldiers, Japanese and administrative officials and their families." [19] A Powell laundry and dry cleaning service was allowed to set up an office within the confines of the camp in order to meet the needs of internees and WRA personnel. The Cody Trading Company had an office in Block 20 where orders were taken for groceries and dry goods with guaranteed delivery within forty-eight hours. Ray Easton, the undertaker in Powell, also saw an increase in business when Heart Mountain, a "community" of nearly 11,000, was located nearby. As the residents of the camp were allowed to apply for passes to shop in Powell or Cody, local merchants also benefitted greatly. Al Fryer, a Powell merchant, said that by June 1944 the internees were contributing between $25,000 and $50,000 per year to that town's economy. In addition, internees were required to pay Wyoming sales tax on purchases made within the confines of the camp. During the first year of the camp's existence, the residents of Heart Mountain paid $12,260.00 in Wyoming sales taxes. They also paid $1,166.42 in county property taxes. That amount was assessed on unsold goods in the center's canteens. The money collected from property taxes was distributed to the school districts in Park County. [20]

Although many Cody and Powell merchants and businessmen benefitted directly from the Heart Mountain Relocation Center, those who received the greatest benefit were area farmers. It can be argued that the Japanese who worked the beet fields were paid the prevailing wage, but had the internees not been willing to go out and participate in the harvest, it is more than likely that a substantial part of the 1942 and 1943 sugar beet and bean crops would have rotted in the fields. This is true not only for the Powell and Cody area, but for the states of Montana, Wyoming, Idaho, Utah, Colorado and Nebraska. [21]

Big Horn Basin area farmers had been discussing the labor shortage as early as August. As the evacuees began arriving at Heart Mountain, pressure was building on the WRA to allow the Japanese to leave camp and work in the beet fields. Joseph H. Smart, WRA Regional Director in Denver, said evacuees would be made available, on a volunteer basis, to area farmers, but that certain qualifications had first to be met. Farmers had to fill out request forms stating what kind of labor was to be done, how many workers would be needed, what wage the farmer would pay, and what type of housing, if necessary, the laborers would be given. Completed forms were first sent to area employment offices to see if requests could be filled with local laborers. The stumbling block came when Smart said that the governor and local law enforcement officials would be responsible for the security of the laborers and ensuring that the prevailing wage was paid. [22]

Since state and local authorities were to have the responsibility of protecting internees who were working outside the camp, the governor felt he would require some control over the workers. Smith said he wanted the power to terminate working agreements with the evacuees when "in his judgement, the welfare of the communities, or of the State of Wyoming, can best be served by the return of the Japanese to their relocation centers." [23]

Governor Nels Smith (center) discusses labor situation with Assistant Director Guy Robertson (right) (JR-BSC).

While Smith was standing firm on his requirements for allowing the Japanese to leave Heart Mountain on work passes, he was contacted by Holly Sugar Company, Great Western Sugar Company, the National Beet Growers Association, the Montana-Wyoming Beet Growers Association, the Wyoming USDA War Board and a number of other groups and individuals, including W. J. Gorst of Worland who had stated earlier that he did not want the Japanese in Wyoming and did not need them to work the beet fields. All of these companies and individuals wanted the governor to make whatever arrangements were necessary to allow laborers from Heart Mountain to help bring in the crops as soon as possible. [24]

There were delays in getting laborers into the fields despite pressure from the previously mentioned groups. Smith did not feel that as governor he could allow the release of Japanese in Wyoming without restrictions and guarantees as to when they would be returned to the camp. The governor wanted some control over the situation but was informed by Joseph Smart that no state official would be allowed to dictate WRA policy. Smart agreed that the volunteer laborers would be returned to camp if the governor felt it necessary, but he would not allow it to be printed in any labor contracts. Smith's concern was that once the Japanese were released to work in the fields, they would not go back to camp, but would instead establish permanent residence in Wyoming. [25]

While the governor was concerned with his control over the farm labor situation, Senator O'Mahoney was being flooded with telegrams explaining the farmers' position. The most urgent requests were coming from Sheridan and Johnson Counties. The telegrams were all very similar. There were requests for 300 laborers, asking that everything possible be done to gain the release of workers from Heart Mountain. The farmers felt that crops could not be harvested without Japanese labor. Some of them were to the point of begging that some kind of arrangement be worked out with the governor because laborers were so desperately needed. [26]

The farmers, however, were put on hold by the governor while Senator O'Mahoney tried to work out a deal between Dillon S. Myer, Milton Eisenhower's successor as Director of the WRA, and Governor Smith. The governor said that it was his intention to help Wyoming farmers get the labor they needed to harvest the crops. But he added that the people of Wyoming did not want the state, or any section of it, permanently populated with West Coast Japanese. Before he allowed laborers to leave Heart Mountain, Smith wanted "some assurance that the Japanese will be reassembled at the relocation center when their services are no longer needed for the emergency." [27]

C. E. Rachford, director of the Heart Mountain Relocation Center, had requests for 2,000 laborers as early as September 1, 1942, but an agreement between Governor Smith and the WRA was not reached until September 21. During that two-week period, the more experienced internees, as far as sugar beet work was concerned, left Heart Mountain to work in Montana. Smith's attempts to keep some sort of control over the labor situation cost Wyoming farmers three weeks of valuable time. The result was that once laborers were allowed to leave Heart Mountain to work in the fields of Wyoming beet growers, those farmers often received workers with little or no experience. [28] When he ran for reelection two months later, Smith was defeated by Democrat Lester Hunt. The dissatisfaction of Wyoming farmers and others in the state trying to acquire laborers from Heart Mountain was certainly a factor in Smith's inability to retain office.

Senator O'Mahoney, on the other hand, was contacted by a number of people in farm related industries thanking him for his help in regard to the labor problem. One such individual was P. B. Smith, the plant manager for Great Western Sugar Company in Lovell, Wyoming. Mr. Smith thanked O'Mahoney for helping area farmers to secure the needed labor and added that, "Most of the Japanese appear to be very fine people. . . ." [29]

Despite the profound labor shortage, Heart Mountain internees could not be forced to leave camp to work. Sixty-three percent of Heart Mountain's prospective labor force was made up of American citizens, and federal law prohibited the drafting of Americans for labor projects against their will. Furthermore, under the dictates of the Geneva Convention, Japanese aliens, those "ineligible to citizenship," could not be forced to work either. Therefore, all labor was voluntary. In spite of objections by local farmers who felt they should be able to hire all of the labor they could afford, workers from the camp were distributed to farming areas according to the number of acres planted. The worker distribution formula and Governor Smith's holdout for a satisfactory agreement, which resulted in laborers being held in camp until late in the season, led to many complaints from Wyoming farming communities. [30]

The Sheridan County Beet Growers Association felt that it was extremely unfair that Japanese laborers from Heart Mountain had to be shared with farmers in Montana and Nebraska. [31] According to W. E. Pearson, president of the First National Bank in Lovell, the beet harvest was being impaired by a continuing labor shortage. He said that businessmen and high school students were all working in the beet fields, and claimed that out of 12,000 Japanese at Heart Mountain only 1050 were working. "In this emergency they are being mollycoddled by relocation authorities. If they are American citizens they should accept the same responsibilities as the rest of us . . . ." [32] In spite of Pearson's complaints, Lovell Mayor Frank Brown called on city officials, citizens and law enforcement officers "to maintain such peace and harmony and see that the said Japanese laborers are treated with every form of courtesy and protection due a citizen of the United States." [33] It was not long before Lovell became a favorite destination of Heart Mountain sports teams, swing bands, orchestras and laborers.

WRA Regional Director, Joseph Smart, told Senator O'Mahoney to have Pearson visit the center where he could get the correct figures which would answer his criticisms. Smart said that there were 510 evacuees working in Wyoming and 653 working in Montana with a few in Nebraska as of October 14, 1942. Director Myer added that that number of laborers came from a population at Heart Mountain, as of October 21, of 9,757, not 12,000. By the end of the harvest season, nearly 1,400 evacuees from the camp were working under farm labor contracts. [34] Neither WRA official was very receptive to Pearson's ill informed accusations. It is interesting that throughout the relocation years, individuals like W. E. Pearson continually came forward to cite the obligations of incarcerated citizens, having experienced none of the relocation process for themselves.

Despite a number of problems and complaints, the 1942 beet crop was brought in without much trouble. S. B. Smith, of Great Western Sugar Company in Lovell, reported that by mid December 112,000 tons of beets had been refined. He added that 400 volunteers from Heart Mountain helped with the crop at various stages, and that, while for the most part, they were inexperienced in the sugar beet business, they learned quickly and made excellent workers. [35]

While area farmers worried about their crops, and others concerned themselves with the economic benefits they might reap from Heart Mountain, the evacuees were trying to settle in. The relocation center was far from complete when its new residents arrived.

Chapter V

Arriving at Heart Mountain

The first residents of Heart Mountain were expected to arrive sometime in mid August even though the camp, with all of its "modern conveniences," which was thrown together in sixty days' time was not yet complete. R. T. Baird, editor of the *Powell Tribune*, said that "Engineers planning the new Heart Mountain city chose a most attractive site."[1] It was in a "beautiful" area near the eastern base of Heart Mountain.[2]

Internees arriving at Heart Mountain (JR-BSC).

On August 11 the first evacuees arrived at Heart Mountain just after midnight (the WRA's official date for the opening of the camp was August 12). The first arrivals were internees who had volunteered to come to camp early to help get things ready for those who followed. Ben Okura, one of the first arrivals, described the camp as, "pretty spooky." It reminded him of a giant ghost town. Okura had a number of jobs associated with the preparations being made at Heart Mountain.

He delivered army cots and mattresses (not the straw-stuffed mattresses used at assembly centers) to the empty barracks and filled barrels at the end of each building with water for fire fighting purposes. The fire hydrants, as with many other essentials, had yet to be installed. Okura later drove a truck picking up evacuees at the railroad siding and delivering them to their barracks. [3]

Internees and their belongings being loaded onto trucks for the one mile drive to the camp (JR-BSC).

There were other internees who arrived early to help with the settlement of new residents and the completion of construction projects in the camp. Kakuchi Araki carried out many of the same jobs as Ben Okura. Bill Hosokawa, who in a short time became editor of the *Heart Mountain Sentinel*, the camp newspaper, worked with one of the center's senior administrative officials, John Nelson, checking new arrivals into camp as they departed from the trains. Hosokawa was sent to Heart Mountain from the assembly center at Puyallup, Washington, where he was seen as a potential, "disruptive element," while his parents were sent to the Minidoka Relocation Center in Idaho. [4]

The situation became hectic as train loads of evacuees began to arrive and attempts were made to settle people into their barracks as quickly as possible. The internees' first impressions of Heart Mountain differed sharply from those of R. T. Baird who described it as an "attractive site" in a "beautiful area." The observations made by the new arrivals were unanimous. The consensus was that the camp and the surrounding area were "barren, desolate, flat open desert, bleak, scrubby, lonely, dusty and a plain of sagebrush with not a tree in sight." [5]

Others gave more detailed descriptions of their first impressions of Heart Mountain. The landscape reminded Yosh Sogioka of the Indian country he had seen in cowboy movies as a child. Ruth Hashimoto said she and many others "shed bitter tears" when they saw what was to be their new home. Rose (Tsuneishi) Yamashiro described the area in the same manner as other new arrivals, but she also took a look in the mirror. She said that evacuees must have been a sight to see, all of those black haired people in dusty old trains arriving in Wyoming in September with no warm clothing. [6] Since the evacuees were not informed as to their final destination until just prior to leaving the assembly centers, they had no time to prepare for life in Wyoming and its climate. The surplus navy pea-coats which the WRA issued were only a slight help against the cold.

Internees walking toward their new homes (JR-BSC).

Others were too worried or sick to take immediate note of their new surroundings. When Ada Endo arrived, she was deeply concerned for her seven-month-old son, Douglas, who had been very sick the greater part of the journey from Santa Anita to Heart Mountain. An ambulance met the train at the camp and transported Douglas to the relocation center's hospital. Another evacuee was in a hospital in California with a serious heart ailment when he was told to prepare to leave for Wyoming. Despite his condition, officials in California loaded the man on a train and sent him to Heart Mountain. In Cheyenne he was taken from the train to a hotel room where he received medical attention. Within a short period of time, he was placed back on the train for the continuation of his journey. According to administrator John Nelson, an ambulance was sent to meet the train in Deaver, Wyoming so that the man could at least make that much of the trip (25 miles) lying down. Nelson said that on its face, the entire episode was nothing more than an attempt at "premeditated murder."[7]

One month after the camp opened, the population of Heart Mountain reached 6,281. Before the new residents could settle into any sort of routine, however, they first had to make their "modern accommodations" livable. Each barrack building was 120 feet long and 20 feet wide. The building was then divided into six single room "apartments." The size of the rooms varied. The 20x24 foot rooms were for large families of up to six people, and sometimes more. The 20x20 foot rooms were for smaller families of up to four individuals, and the 20x16 foot rooms for smaller groups yet. Each room had a pot-belly stove for heat (not all stoves were installed when evacuees first arrived) and a single light hanging from the open rafters.[8]

Toshiko (Nagamori) Ito said each barrack room was covered with dust. As in the assembly centers, the walls of barracks at Heart Mountain were constructed with green lumber which shrank as it dried. With no insulation on the inside of

Mr. and Mrs. Nagamori in front of their barracks apartment. Mr. Nagamori was amazed at how well his flower garden grew in Wyoming (JTIC).

the walls, the tar-paper nailed to the outside of the buildings did little to hold the weather out. Dirt from the frequent dust storms blew right through the barracks. In the Nagamori apartment, as in others, the windows were crooked, could barely be opened, and did not close tightly; the door was put on in such a manner that it would not close tightly. Mr. Nagamori made repairs with tools ordered from the Sears & Roebuck catalogue. [9]

Other evacuees described the barracks in a similar fashion. The housing was minimal at best. Ropes were tied to the rafters and sheets hung to the floor for some semblance of privacy. Newspapers and rags, stuffed into the spaces between the wall boards, failed to keep out the dust and cold. Jean Ushijima said that she spent a great deal of her time at Heart Mountain sweeping, as the dirt continually filtered through the walls. [10] A Cody women visiting the camp as the internees arrived said she "could see out of almost every apartment by merely looking through cracks in the wall." [11] The barracks were more of a "work in progress" than a completed home, with internees continuing to make improvements over the years.

By the beginning of October, the population of Heart Mountain had surpassed the 10,000 mark. At that time, construction was still on going. Some of the latrines had not yet been completed, and some stoves in the apartments were not yet insulated and could not be used. Celotex was eventually put on all of the apartment walls in an effort to keep the dirt, wind and cold out, and was nailed to the rafters to form a ceiling for warmth and privacy. The celotex was put up by the internees themselves using the tools they purchased from Sears and Montgomery Ward. However, the celotex did not arrive at Heart Mountain until December, well into what became one of the coldest Wyoming winters on record. [12]

The single light bulb dangling from the rafters in the center of the room and the army cots and mattresses, along with the stove for heating the apartments, were the only furnishings the new arrivals had. A few internees had household items sent to them by friends back home or from places where they had put belongings into storage. The large majority of the residents built their own furniture. Scraps of lumber left over from the main construction phase of the project were used to make furniture for the apartments, in addition to room dividers and in some instances, shutters for the windows. Other items that could not be built with the materials at hand were ordered from Sears or Montgomery Ward and paid for by the internees themselves. Mike Hatchimonji and his family often referred to the Sears catalogue as the "Bible," due to its importance in their lives at camp. [13]

While the barracks lacked any furnishings other than cots and stoves, some did not even possess those. Evacuees were arriving at a rate faster than they could be accommodated, and supplies were short. On September 13, two trains arrived carrying more than 1,000 internees. Due to a shortage of cots, blankets and completed accommodations, one wing of the hospital was opened for women and children to stay in. Despite that, WRA employee, Frank Cross, said that "many of the arrivals were forced to walk the streets all night without protection from the cold." [14] Ed Sakauye and his family arrived on the thirteenth and were shown to their apartment. There were no cots or mattresses, only a pot-bellied stove. But since there was no coal for the stove, the family huddled together in the center of the room to try to keep warm. [15]

Trying to get enough to eat was also a problem. Nearly all of the evacuees complained about the quantity and quality of the food. It was generally described as "fair to poor in quality. . . ." [16] There were few if any prayers of thanks for what they were given to eat. John Nelson, one of the camp administrators, said he would not have been surprised if trouble erupted in camp over the food situation. On August 30, a large group of internees eating at one mess hall became violently ill and had to be hospitalized. On September 11, one of the mess halls reported that there was not enough food for everyone at dinner and nothing to serve for breakfast the next day. The people at that dining facility had been eating frankfurters for three days. At another mess hall a few days earlier, 150 workers were fed "a half wiener and small amount of potatoe [sic] each." [17]

Two factors figured into the food problem. The first was supply. Although a few mess halls had more food than they needed, others were badly under supplied, and it was not until January 1943 that all residents were adequately fed. This meant that some people were going hungry as individuals were required to eat in specific mess halls. Early on, young people would often go from one mess hall to the next in order get enough food, or the best food. The evacuee cooks in the mess halls wanted to speak with the chief steward concerning the shortages, but the assistant stewards would not allow it. Finally, in desperation, one of the cooks attempted to "carve-up" the assistant steward in his mess hall. The cook said later that he thought if the assistant steward was injured someone in the administration might pay attention to the problem. [18]

When the camp's Internal Security people looked into the case and asked the project steward his point of view in the matter, he said that the mess halls were being run in a good manner and that the complaints were being lodged by a "disgruntled minority." Mr. Takeda, the cook who threatened to carve-up the assistant steward, was asked his opinion of the problem. Takeda pointed out, quite correctly, that Mr. Hawes, the project steward, and his assistants had no idea of what was involved in an operation of this size or in the feeding of so many people. Hawes attempted to remedy the situation by calling a meeting of all the cooks and explaining to them the proper procedure for requesting food and supplies. While the cooks were filling out food requisition forms and waiting for them to be processed, people were going hungry. The meeting did not alleviate the problem, and in the meantime, another assistant steward by the name of Best was attacked by a disgruntled and exasperated cook (Best figured prominently in later accusations against the camp). [19]

Camp Director, C. E. Rachford, made up excuses for his inept project steward, but the inability to handle the mess hall situation and other problems which arose in the future, were not entirely the fault of Heart Mountain administrators. Though a comparison can be made to the operation of some Indian reservations, running a concentration camp in America was a new experience. And as is often typical of the government, it simply moved bureaucrats from one position to another whether they had any experience in the new job or not. Rachford had just recently retired as an assistant chief of the United States Forest Service when Milton Eisenhower called him back into service for the WRA. Rachford reported for work at the Tule Lake camp in California in June of 1942 but left after only one week, opting for the job at Heart Mountain instead. [20]

Although Rachford supported his chief steward, he did agree with internee representatives that an impartial investigation of the mess hall situation was warranted. Nine male teachers (Caucasian) were appointed to head the investigation. These investigators found that the problem lay solely within the administration and that changes had to be made. The two cooks who attacked the assistant stewards were relieved of their duties. Following the investigation, project steward Hawes, and a few months later, Mr. Best, were replaced. [21]

The second problem with the mess hall system was with the cooks

Heart Mountain mess hall. Drawing by Estelle Ishigo (BSC).

themselves. Frank Hayami said that some cooks were very good while others were amateurs who just wanted that particular job. According to Hayami, the mess hall in Block 8 had one of the worst teams of cooks in camp. The combination of poor quality food and bad cooks drove those who were forced to eat in the Block 8 mess hall to call a meeting. At the meeting, the original cooks were fired and a new team was brought in. The quality of meals improved almost immediately. The Block 20 mess hall was apparently the envy of most of the camp. The cooks, according to Hayami, had worked at an oriental restaurant in Los Angeles. Those cooks, from the "San Kwo Low" restaurant, "took the same ingredients furnished to all mess halls and turned them into things of delight." [22]

While the WRA and the Heart Mountain camp administrators were trying to iron out the problems of housing and feeding the new arrivals, there were other projects which they wanted to get underway in an effort to give the internees some sense of community. Creating a typical American community at Heart Mountain was impossible. It would have been naive, to say the least, for camp officials to believe that they could take more than 10,000 people who had been forcibly uprooted from their homes, businesses and lifestyles against their will, place them behind barbed wire, and then expect them to act as though they were part of a normal American community. But the WRA tried to come as close as possible. The administration felt that a group of people who believed they had some say in their future would be easier to control.

John Nelson felt that a system of government was needed as soon as possible. That government, he believed, would at least give the people a type of grievance committee which could present evacuee complaints to the administration. A short time later, as each block was filled by the incoming internees, the administration appointed temporary Block Chairmen. The chairmen held regular block meetings, and during the first month met daily with the administration to iron out such problems as food and housing. The chairmen became the main line of communication between administrators and residents. In fact, the administration referred to the chairmen as "shock absorbers." [23]

Each block consisted of approximately 500 residents. From that group, a block committee was elected, and in the early days of the camp's existence, meetings were held every Monday. The chairmen, who had been appointed on a temporary basis, asked for confirmation of their positions by a vote of evacuees living within their block. All but one of the chairmen were given the support of the blocks they represented. The administration later appointed Block Managers who were to see to it that administration policy was carried out. The chairmen were, for the most part, "Issei," while the Block Managers were "Nisei." The powers of the chairmen and managers often overlapped and residents did not see a need for both. [24]

The administration's insistence on both chairmen and managers caused some conflict between the two. By December, however, the managers were told to tend to administrative duties and stay out of block politics. Unofficially, they did as they wished. The administration was pushing for the adoption of a camp charter and a permanent government by the end of November 1942. The evacuees, both Issei and Nisei, who had been enthusiastic about the government system, began to see the camp charter as the WRA's, and not their own. The charter was not approved, nor was a "permanent" government established until August 1943. [25]

The establishment of a system of government did bring the evacuees together and helped in their realizing that sought-after "sense of community." Historian Douglas Nelson described community government at Heart Mountain as a farce. Bill Hosokawa said the internees knew that. "Have you ever heard of democratic self-government behind the barbed wire of a prison camp?" The internees understood that the final word on anything came from the Project Director, C. E. Rachford, and after December 15, 1942 when Rachford retired, Guy Robertson, the new camp director, or Dillon Myer, head of the WRA in Washington. Hosokawa added that the community government went through the motions, and the evacuees took what they could get. Administrative officials pointed out that the community government was instrumental in solving the mess hall and other problems. [26] While the community government did not have absolute control over the internees' future, it was able to present grievances to the administration in a manner which did not appear threatening or demanding. Nelson was wrong to write off the whole process as an insignificant farce. He is correct in pointing out that by end of 1944 "only 8 candidates filed for the twenty seats on the community council." [27] However, Nelson fails to mention that by the end of 1944 the population at Heart Mountain had significantly decreased, and it was quite apparent that the camps would be closed in the near future as internees would be allowed to return to the West Coast.

Another important factor in giving the new arrivals at Heart Mountain a sense of community was the establishment of a camp newspaper. The first day Bill Hosokawa arrived at camp he met Vaughn Mechau, a one-time newspaper man who was part of the center's administration. One of Mechau's assignments was to organize a camp newspaper. To that end, Hosokawa and Mechau met with Jack Richard, editor of the *Cody Enterprise*, to discuss the newspaper prospect at Heart Mountain. Richard said he could locate enough newsprint for 6,000 copies of an eight-page weekly paper. The paper could then be printed at the *Enterprise* offices in Cody. [28]

Hosokawa, who became the founding editor of the camp's newspaper, the *Heart Mountain Sentinel*, was told by Mechau that he would have to start the paper himself. Fortunately, Hosokawa had experience with that type of daunting task. With a degree in journalism from the University of Washington, and little likelihood that as a Japanese American he would be able to land a newspaper job on the West Coast, Hosokawa, in 1938 took a job in Singapore where, working for a Japanese businessman, he established an English-language newspaper, the

Singapore Herald. Hosokawa's experience with the *Herald*, and his ability to tap experienced journalists in camp, made the *Heart Mountain Sentinel* the most professionally run, and edited, of the ten relocation center newspapers. [29]

The first edition of the *Sentinel* came out on October 24, 1942. From that date, the paper was distributed every Saturday until the summer of 1945 when it discontinued service as the camp was slowly closing operations. The *Sentinel* originally sold for three cents per copy, but that was reduced to two cents a short time later. Hosokawa felt the paper was important because it gave the residents of Heart Mountain a means of expression and allowed them to blow off steam. Space was made in the *Sentinel* in the letters to the editor column and in a column titled, "I'd like to see." In addition to offering this forum for community opinion, Hosokawa said the paper printed the news and offered editorial leadership. [30]

To keep all of the residents of Heart Mountain informed, the *Sentinel* also ran a Japanese language edition, since nearly one-third of the camp's residents were Issei. Kohay Washizuka and a number of others translated the *Sentinel* into Japanese for those who could not read English. The translation work was all done by hand as there was no means of printing kanji (Chinese characters) or katakana and hiragana (Japanese characters used in combination with kanji). Through the hard work of Hosokawa, Imura, Washizuka and other staff members like John Kitasako, Louise Suski, Kara Kondo and Michi Onuma, the *Sentinel* became a source of pride at Heart Mountain. Approximately 4,500 of the 6,000 copies of the *Sentinel* which were published each week were sent by individual subscribers to friends and relatives outside the camp. [31]

In October of 1943, Bill Hosokawa and his family relocated from Heart Mountain to Des Moines, Iowa. Hosokawa had accepted a job with the *Des Moines Register*, leaving managing editor Haruo Imura to take over operation of the *Sentinel*. Though working full-time for the *Register*, Hosokawa continued to write a weekly column for the *Sentinel* in which he informed the camp's readers about life on the outside and kept them abreast of events which had any bearing on the lives and future of those still behind barbed wire. [32]

With the housing and food problems being taken care of and the establishment of the camp newspaper, internees began to develop some sense of community. Though there were other issues still to be faced, evacuees started to settle into a daily routine. However, the residents soon found dealing with everyday life in the camp a struggle.

Chapter VI

Everyday Life in the Center

Life in the Heart Mountain Relocation Center was a monotonous grind. Most of the internees worked either inside the camp or for area farmers and businessmen on the outside. The bean and sugar beet crops kept the majority of those who worked outside the camp busy, at least during the autumn months. Aside from harvesting, there was thinning and processing to be done. Some of the residents worked for a number of the different railroads in the West and Midwest. A few internees worked in the near-by communities of Powell and Cody as domestics while others labored for area businesses. One young internee worked for the Shoshone Irrigation District in Deaver. The young man, who enjoyed the job, said the Caucasian employees who couldn't pronounce his name, just called him "Shoshone."[1]

Arthur Ishigo worked as Block 14s hot water boiler man (BSC).

Yosh Sogioka worked for a Park County construction contractor, Taggart-Smith Construction Company of Cody. The work not only kept Sogioka busy, it gave him a first-hand view of what some in the area surrounding the camp thought about the influx of Japanese people into the county. He felt that many of those on the outside actually believed they would see thousands of buck-toothed, slant-

45

eyed people with thick glasses. Work was one way of coping with the boredom of camp life and of keeping one's mind off all he or she was forced to leave behind. [2]

When they were not working, the internees had numerous activities to help keep them occupied. However, those activities took place within the confines of the camp, or the immediate area surrounding the center. In time, even the activities became boring and monotonous, especially during the winter months. Young mothers were probably some of the busiest people in camp. They seldom had time to be bored or to think of home. As all mothers know, taking care of young children was a full-time job. Caring for children at Heart Mountain was even more difficult. Young mothers like Ada Endo and Emi Kuromiya, both of whom gave birth to children inside the camp, were constantly on the go. [3]

Sets Murakami and son Richard, August 1942 (JR-BSC).

The young women from California soon found that diapers had to be dried inside the barracks during most of the year. Ada Endo said she was quite surprised the first time she went to get the diapers off the line outside and found them frozen. The laundry area, toilets, showers, and mess halls, could be anywhere from forty feet to one city block away from the barracks. The children had to be bundled up and taken along on what was anywhere from five to fifteen trips per day outside the apartment to the different facilities. Or a neighbor had to be found to watch the children while the mother was gone. Children could not be left alone for even a minute due to the fire danger which existed. [4]

46

Fire was one of the greatest dangers internees faced. Most had never seen coal, or a pot-bellied stove. A number of the stoves had not been installed by the time the evacuees arrived at camp. The last stoves installed were sometimes put in in a quick and haphazard manner. They were often too close to the walls and not insulated with enough asbestos. (Today asbestos is seen as a major health hazard.) Since the residents were from California, they were not accustomed to using heating devices of that type. One internee, and he was likely not alone in his actions, would light a match and throw it into the stove while simultaneously jumping backward, expecting instantaneous combustion. Once the coal was burning, stoves were often overheated. The construction of the buildings also contributed to fire danger. They were nothing more than wood and tar paper and would go up in a matter of minutes if they caught fire. Another construction problem was the wiring. With only one outlet per apartment, the electrical lines were often overloaded. The problem was compounded when some residents replaced blown fuses with pennies. [5]

Barracks building catches fire. Ethel Ryan collection, John Taggart Hinckley Library, Northwest College, Powell, Wyoming, hereafter cited as (ERC).

The Heart Mountain Fire Department was organized on September 1, 1942 and was made up of evacuees who had worked in fire protection at the assembly centers. The Heart Mountain firemen often amazed the camp administrators by fighting fires when it was thirty degrees below zero, and the situation looked hopeless. Internees had already been forced to leave behind their personal belongings once, and fire fighters were determined that residents would not lose what little they still possessed. The firemen still had problems that first year. The water system in the camp was constructed without expansion joints in the lines. During that first winter, one of the coldest on record in Wyoming, the water lines broke continually as pipes froze solid. On those cold winter nights, a fire was kept burning in the apartment stoves, which posed a potential hazard. Volunteers walked a fire-watch in groups of two patrolling outside the barracks on two-hour shifts. [6]

The Heart Mountain Firemen took pride in their work and fought to save everything they could when a fire did start. Very few residents of the camp lost their remaining possessions to fire. One of the few fires which gutted an entire barracks took place in a building which housed Caucasian administrative personnel. The fire destroyed the entire building. The internees who belonged to the Community Christian Church at Heart Mountain took up a collection and raised $35 which was turned over to the victims of the fire. A short time later, the victims donated $34 to the Heart Mountain Fire Department for its courageous effort in battling the blaze. [7]

Heart Mountain firefighters in action (ERC).

The hospital at Heart Mountain also played an important role in everyday life. The medical facility was staffed by doctors from among the internees. The nurses were both internees and Caucasians brought in from the outside, while nurses' aides came from the resident population. Trying to paint a positive picture, the *Heart Mountain Sentinel*, on October 31, 1942, described the hospital as one of the best in Wyoming. However, such was not the case. Dr. Charles Irwin, the chief medical officer, was forced to buy what supplies he could on the local market, while sending patients requiring surgery to Powell, Cody, or as far away as Billings, Montana. [8]

The shortages affected both internees and Caucasian staff alike. Velma Kessel, a Caucasian nurse who lived at Heart Mountain during the week, found that her barrack apartment contained an army cot and a nail keg, which she used as a stool, and nothing else. The hospital itself contained no beds or cribs. The patients were placed on cots. When children were admitted to the hospital, a parent was required to be on hand to keep a younger child in his or her cot. With no soap, wash cloths, or towels, aides gave patients baths using a fire bucket and sponge. The last of delayed supplies arrived early in the spring of 1943 [9]

The Heart Mountain Hospital was a 100 bed facility which could be expanded to 120 beds in an emergency. The hospital had seventeen wings made up of barracks buildings connected by a long hallway. There were nine physicians, eleven dentists, three optometrists, ten registered nurses, forty-nine aides, and ten pharmacists. By April 1943, there was some concern with the medical facilities. The number of doctors had declined to six, and due to the severe winter, all of the beds were filled. Many patients had to be treated at home by the camp's public health nurse and internee aides. [10]

Keeping enough physicians at Heart Mountain was a real concern for administrators throughout the camp's existence. Doctors could relocate to the outside more easily than most residents because they had no trouble finding jobs. The pay for an internee doctor on the outside was also better than the $19 per month they received working in camp alongside a less experienced Caucasian doctor. Velma Kessel's situation illustrates the disparity in pay. As a Caucasian registered nurse with a barrack apartment in camp, Kessel was paid $1,800 per year. Internee doctors, on the other hand, were paid $228 per year, with internee aides and other support staff receiving as little as $12 to $16 per month. [11]

Once properly supplied, the hospital's facilities and its employees were, for the most part, the best around. Ada Endo and Emi Kuromiya were only two of many women who gave birth to children in the Heart Mountain Hospital. Mori Shimada had his appendix removed in the camp hospital, and two of Kohay Washizuka's daughters had their tonsils taken out there. Once the hospital was fully equipped and supplied, evacuees had few complaints about the quality of service or attention they received. [12] "By the middle of 1944, 848 surgeries had been performed at the Heart Mountain Hospital with tonsillectomies and appendectomies being the most frequent." [13]

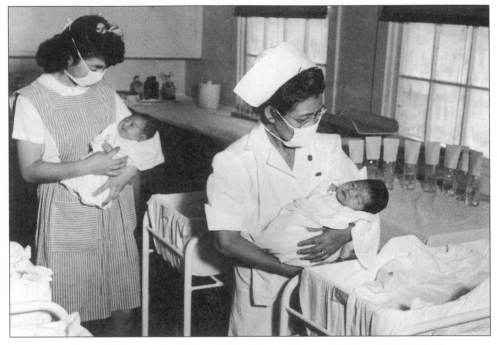

Newborn babies receiving care at the Heart Mountain Hospital (ERC).

There were two ambulances available twenty-four hours a day to pick-up any individual in camp who was too sick to walk to the hospital. Each ambulance was attended by two men who worked in eight-hour shifts. During the spring of 1943, there were an average of 250 ambulance calls per week. However, the ambulance drivers also had other duties. Since there was no refrigeration available in the barracks apartments, formula for new-born babies was made in the hospital kitchen on Ward Eight and delivered by ambulance every four hours. A mother, working through the pediatrician, would inform the hospital how many bottles of formula her child would require in a twenty-four hour period. Once bottles of formula were made-up and addressed, they were delivered, with the empty bottles being picked up. [14]

The most destructive phase of everyday life at Heart Mountain was the institutionalization of the residents, a process which began in the assembly centers. The mess hall was a major factor in that institutionalization. Families were no longer dependent on the head of the household. The WRA provided meals, jobs, and a small clothing allowance. Young people, especially teenagers, no longer depended on their fathers or mothers. This led to a number of problems which resulted from the break-down of the family unit. Toshiko Ito's mother, Mrs. Nagamori, worked in the camp's social welfare office. The most frequent problems she faced involved women who were no longer in need of husbands to provide food and shelter. Teenagers were also a prevalent "problem group." Some families like the Hatchimonjis made trays and containers which would keep food warm and took meals back to their barracks so they could eat as a family. It was more work, but it did help to keep the family together. The problems leading to the breakdown of the family unit were compounded when many of the men left camp to work for the railroads or to labor on farms in other states. Since the work was seasonal, the whole family did not relocate. [15]

Japanese Americans could apply to leave camp to attend college or move to communities outside the designated defense zones, provided they could find work. This process, known as "relocation," also split up families and scattered them across the country. Yas (Morita) Ikeda's experience was an example of how a family could be split apart. Ikeda's eighteen-year-old brother was in camp only a month when he received a scholarship to attend Heidelberg College in Ohio. Her older brother, who had attended medical school prior to evacuation, worked in the camp hospital for a year before being hired by a hospital in Detroit. Ikeda's sixteen-year-old sister moved to Buffalo, New York, after a year in camp, to live with a family her brother knew. Her father was in and out of camp continuously. The nearly sixty year old Mr. Morita worked topping sugar beets and for the railroads on a seasonal basis. He also left camp in early 1945 for San Francisco to find work and a place for the family to live, once Japanese Americans were cleared to return to the West Coast. [16]

The breakdown of the family unit resulted in the formation of some youth gangs. And there were a few fathers who lost face in the community when an unmarried daughter became pregnant. On occasion, the girl in question was kicked out of the house. Emi Kuromiya said that a neighbor first threw his daughter out and then burned all of her belongings. The girl was taken in by another family. There was no privacy in the camp. Everything was communal. It was virtually impossible to hide wrongdoing, and with the many rumors which circulated through camp, an individual might have been accused of things he or she had never been involved in. [17]

Facing numerous obstacles and problems, the residents of Heart Mountain tried to make the best of the situation in which they found themselves. No matter what happened, life went on. Couples married, and some divorced, babies were born, and people died. Many of those who were married during their incarceration at Heart Mountain had the wedding ceremony performed in Powell or Cody. During the spring of 1943, an average of three couples per week were getting married. Trips were made to Powell or Cody on Wednesdays. In many instances, the couples acted as each others' witnesses. They went to town in a WRA vehicle and were accompanied by a Caucasian camp administrative official. Being married in Powell or Cody instead of in camp served a number of purposes. It was a way for the young couple to get out of the center and into town. In addition, it enabled the couple to avoid a large family wedding. Having the ceremony in Powell or Cody also eliminated the stigma of being married within the barbed wire confines of a concentration camp. [18]

Despite problems which occurred with the breakdown of the family unit, only seven couples discussed divorce with the camp attorney while living at Heart Mountain. Of that number there were only two divorce hearings. It is probable, however, that a number of couples agreed to a divorce without a hearing or consulting the camp attorney. [19]

During the camp's three-year and three-month existence there were 552 births and 183 deaths. The first birth in the camp was a boy born to Mr. and Mrs. Akiyo Miyatani. The baby arrived on September 4, 1942. Those who were born at Heart Mountain came into the world as American citizens behind barbed wire which had been erected by their own government. Mr. T. Okamato's death was the first reported in camp. Okamato died of a brain hemorrhage on August 28, 1942, shortly after his arrival at Heart Mountain. Those who died at Heart Mountain were buried in the camp cemetery if they had a Christian service. If it was a Buddhist ceremony, as most were, the body of the deceased was put on a train and shipped to Great Falls, Montana for cremation. The ashes were then returned to the family. Great Falls, nearly 400 miles north of Heart Mountain, had the closest facilities to perform cremations. [20]

Funeral Service (ERC).

Some cases were more tragic than others. Genichiro Nishiyama died in an accidental fall while dismantling an abandoned CCC camp. He left behind a wife and two children who had to get along and start over without a husband or father. Kojiro Kawakami left the Tule Lake Relocation Center to work in the sugar beet fields of Montana. When he became ill, he was transported to Heart Mountain, which was the closest relocation facility. Kawakami died of pneumonia in the Heart Mountain Hospital on November 1, 1942. After contacting the Tule Lake center and finding no one to claim the body, the sixty-two-year-old Kawakami was laid to rest in the Heart Mountain cemetery. [21] The tragic case of Clarence Uno illustrates how most evacuees supported their country in spite of how they were treated.

Clarence Uno was born in Japan, so when he immigrated to the United States he was ineligible for U. S. citizenship. Despite that fact, Uno, along with several hundred other Japanese, served with the American Expeditionary Forces in France during World War I. Due to his outstanding service in the war, Uno and a number of other Japanese who served were given United States citizenship by a special act of Congress in March of 1936. Uno became involved in the Veterans of Foreign Wars and the American Legion. In January of 1941, Uno was named to the registrants' advisory board in El Monte, California, after President Roosevelt signed the first peace time conscription into law. Clarence Uno could easily have been classified as one of America's most patriotic citizens. [22]

Despite his patriotism and service to the country, Uno and his family were incarcerated behind barbed wire with all of the other Japanese and Japanese Americans who lived within the designated military zones on the West Coast. While that sort of treatment would rightly turn many people against the country and government of the United States, Uno was not discouraged. Heart Mountain was open for less than a month when the rumors of "coddling the Japs" began. On September 9, 1942, a number of American Legion officials from Powell and Cody inspected the camp. They were given a complete tour by Uno, acting commander of the Heart Mountain American Legion Post, and four other Japanese American veterans. [23] In early January 1943, Wyoming Governor Lester Hunt appointed Uno as "an associate member of the registrants' advisory board in Park County." [24] Forced to live behind barbed wire in his own country, Uno nonetheless continued proudly to serve America as best he could.

In late January, 1943, Clarence Uno died of a heart attack at the age of 48. He spent the day before his death working at the Heart Mountain USO. The *Heart Mountain Sentinel* said that Uno's death "was release from confinement, against which he showed no resentment, by a government he loved and served." [25] Clarence Uno was accorded full military honors. The American Legions of Powell, Cody and Heart Mountain all participated at the funeral, and a rifle squad gave the deceased a twenty-one gun salute. Life magazine took photographs of the funeral service but they were not published during the war. [26]

The elderly residents in camp, in most cases, had lost everything they had worked for. Once sent to Heart Mountain the older evacuees had little to look forward to. They remembered their hard work and how they had made a life for themselves on the West Coast. After evacuation, it was all lost. Most of the elderly did not wish to try to relocate, as they did not have the desire to start over again. The young on the other hand, found camp life to be somewhat of an adventure. They had school, Scouting and other activities to keep them busy. Mike Hatchimonji said that people his age (fifteen) did not carry "the emotional baggage of a lost business . . . ." [27] As the young people adapted to camp life, their parents did not bother them with thoughts of what was lost, or their concern with an uncertain future. [28]

That first Christmas behind barbed wire was a difficult time for internees of all ages. Parents who worked in camp received poor wages, and unless they had some savings before they were removed from their homes, the situation looked bleak at Christmas time. The Sears catalogue was again the most important and most popular book in camp. The problem faced by parents who did have some money to spend on their children was whether to buy toys or to order something practical like warm clothing. [29]

Christmas at Heart Mountain (ERC).

Aside from being away from home and remembering all that had been lost, that first Christmas turned out better than had been expected. The American Friends Society (the Quakers) and other church groups sent gifts to people (mostly the children) in the camps. Ada Endo said that those gifts restored her faith in people. She was at the point where she believed there was no one on the outside who cared about them. Some gifts also came from people on the West Coast who had not forgotten about their neighbors. A Catholic church in a remote part of New Mexico sent a few gifts and a number of letters. One of the letters was what Kara Kondo referred to as the "Greatest Gift." The letter was from a young girl who said that her priest told the people that there were many children who had been taken from their homes and put in camps behind barbed wire. The priest said they were collecting money to buy a few gifts for the children in those camps. The little girl explained that her family had no money, but that her father had given a few of their chickens to the priest to sell so they could help buy gifts for those in the camps. [30]

Many of those who were sent to Heart Mountain were there for at least three years before they relocated or were allowed to return to the West Coast. The internees adapted as best they could to their situation, and life went on behind barbed wire.

Chapter VII

Education in Camp

While internees were coping with the problems of proper food and housing, another concern was that of the education of their children. In early August of 1942, project director, C. E. Rachford, hired a superintendent of education and a high school principal for the Heart Mountain school system. The two men, Superintendent Clifford D. Carter, and Principal John Corbett, reported to work at Heart Mountain a week before the first evacuees arrived. Both men were experienced Wyoming educators and administrators. Carter had just served eight years as superintendent of the Torrington, Wyoming School District while Corbett had served six years as the principal of Lingle High School. [1]

Upon arrival at Heart Mountain, Carter and Corbett undertook the tasks of developing a curriculum and hiring teachers. Carter contacted Civil Service officials in Denver as he began his search for qualified teachers. Although the teachers would be Civil Service employees paid by the federal government, they had to meet certification requirements of the Wyoming State Board of Education. As Carter began his daunting task of locating and hiring qualified teachers on short notice, additional problems cropped up. Wyoming Congressman, John J. McIntyre, complained that the wages paid to WRA teachers at Heart Mountain were too high, and that Carter was trying to lure qualified instructors away from other communities in Wyoming to teach in the camp. Regional Director Joseph Smart told McIntyre that a high school teacher at Heart Mountain was to receive $2,000 per year for a twelve month contract, which required the teacher to be at work in the camp all year round. Wyoming teachers at a school of comparable size, Laramie was given as an example, received $1,920 for a nine month contract. McIntyre was not concerned with the fact that internee teachers like Takeyoshi Kawahara, who held a master's degree and California teaching certificate, would only receive $228 per year. When Kawahara complained to the United States Commissioner of Education about the disparity in pay, he received a short note explaining that his pay was equal to that of other internee professionals. [2]

By September 30, most of the teachers had been hired, many of them having been recruited in Wyoming and Nebraska that first year. In following years, however, teachers were brought in from Montana and Colorado because of complaints like that lodged by Congressman McIntyre. The vast majority of the teachers at Heart Mountain were Caucasian. However, there were never enough teachers to fill all of the positions available. Nationally, public schools saw a ratio of slightly more than twenty-nine students per teacher. The ratio in the relocation centers was forty-eight to one in the elementary schools and fifty to one in the secondary school. At Heart Mountain High School, for example, a faculty of thirty-seven teachers was approved. But when school opened, there were only thirty, twenty-six Caucasians and four internees. The four internee teachers at the high school and four at the elementary school were granted Wyoming teaching certificates. However, unlike the certificate given to the Caucasian teachers, those granted to internees were stamped, "Valid at Heart Mountain Only." Caucasian teachers, on the other hand, could use their certificates anywhere in Wyoming. This discriminatory action by the Wyoming Board of Education caused a great deal of discontent among the internee teachers. [3] In spite of the Board's action, an editorial in the *Heart Mountain Sentinel* urged the teachers to "accept this discrimination for the sake of the school children." [4]

All of the teachers worked together to help develop a curriculum that they felt would best benefit the students and meet the approval of the state board of education. Developing a curriculum was a small task compared to what the teachers and administrators still faced. As a result of evacuation, students had been removed from the schools they were attending at mid-term. And when students were ready to begin classes at Heart Mountain, no records from their previous schools accompanied them. Without adequate data, the students could be placed in specific grades only after completion of the Stanford, Terman-McNemar Test, and individual interviews with the principal. Elementary school students were given the Kuhlmann-Anderson Intelligence Test. [5]

Elementary school classroom (ERC).

In spite of the fact that there was no school facility *per se*, classes began on October 5, 1942 in temporary quarters. The administration set aside five barracks buildings, each containing six rooms, to be used as classrooms. The classrooms were a typical barrack apartment. There was no ceiling, so the lessons from one classroom were a constant interruption in adjoining rooms. With only the single light hanging from the rafters in the center of the room, the classrooms were often too dark. The other problem was heat. There was no insulation in the rooms, and a constant draft came through the spaces between the wall boards. Yas Ikeda said that those who sat next to the stove were too hot and those who sat in the back were constantly cold. [6]

Although it was difficult to contend with the poor classroom conditions, it was the complete lack of equipment which caused the greatest problems. Teachers used wooden crates for desks. Students had no desks. They sat on benches constructed in the camp's carpenter shop. Even if there had been desks available for the students, inadequate classroom size would have prevented their use. By the first of October, a week prior to the commencement of classes, there were still no textbooks. When books did arrive, there were only enough for one class through most of that first year. For example, a chemistry teacher might have received fifty textbooks for five to six sections of the class. Therefore those fifty books would have to serve 200 to 250 students. If a student had homework, he or she would have to return to the class after school and check out the required textbook. In addition to the lack of desks and books, pencils and paper were in short supply. [7]

Some improvements were made during that first year. Celotex finally arrived in December, and the class rooms were insulated. A number of "real blackboards" were delivered to the schools. Prior to their arrival, a typical classroom blackboard was a piece of plywood painted black. The inadequacy of the barracks being used for classrooms was acknowledged immediately not only by the school administrators, but also by the camp administration. In October of 1942 Ben Lummis, a WRA engineer, announced plans for the construction of a new high school and two elementary schools. Construction was begun on the high school that year, and it was completed for the 1943/44 school year. But as a result of newspaper articles outside the camp and complaints that the government was "pampering the Japs," the projects for the construction of two elementary schools were canceled. [8]

During the first year of classes it was clear that many, though not all, of the Caucasian teachers believed that the residents of Heart Mountain belonged in the camp. That belief, on occasion, resulted in friction between Caucasian and internee teachers and teaching assistants. There was also friction between the Caucasian teachers themselves. The vast majority of teachers lived in Cody or Powell. When they boarded a bus for the ride home, the instructors living in camp were left to oversee the after school activities of students. Despite many differences between teachers and students, and between the teachers themselves, by the close of school that first year, students and teachers had become acquainted, and the schools at Heart Mountain began to function as other "normal" schools in Wyoming.[9]

The new high school, said to have been the best built building in the camp, was constructed by the internees themselves, supervised and working with Bennett & Lewis Contractors of Billings, Montana. In fact, since the WRA did not have any engineers on staff at Heart Mountain, the high school heating system was designed by one of the internees. Tatsu Hori was an engineer at the Stanford Research Institute prior to evacuation and developed the entire system. The high school had thirty-nine classrooms, a gymnasium/auditorium and a number of other rooms for office space. The building was also used in the teaching of adult education classes, and the gymnasium became central in importance for school and public events. The five existing elementary schools were condensed into two schools, Lincoln and Washington, and were more centrally located within the camp, though still located in barracks buildings.[10]

Play produced in the new high school auditorium (ERC).

The average years of teaching experience of those who taught at Heart Mountain was higher in the high school, and slightly lower in the elementary schools, when compared to other schools throughout Wyoming. Thirty-eight internees served as teaching assistants in the high school and elementary schools. Most were so efficient that the administration never hesitated to use them as substitutes when teachers left for other jobs or to enter into the service. The assistant would teach the class until a replacement could be found for the teacher who left. The turnover rate for both teachers and assistants was extremely high. Internees were joining the army or relocating to other parts of the country for better paying jobs and a life outside the confines of the camp. Caucasian teachers were going into the service or leaving education for higher paying defense industry jobs. Of the original teaching staff that went to work at Heart Mountain in 1942, only one individual remained on staff the entire time the camp was open. [11]

High school basketball game, Rawlins 21, Heart Mountain 19, spring 1945. Photo courtesy of the Yoichi Hosozawa collection, hereafter cited as (YHC).

By the beginning of the second year, there were enough textbooks for all of the students. There were also ample supplies for students for the duration of the camp's existence. The 1943-44 school year was more settled than the first, with a "normal routine" being established. Among other things, that routine included high school sports activities like football and basketball. Heart Mountain competed in those two sports with teams from throughout the Big Horn Basin in Northwest Wyoming and some teams from Southern Montana. Although the high school basketball team won only about fifty percent of its games, the football team lost only once in two years. That loss was a 19 to 13 thriller against Casper. Leroy Pierce, Casper's 210-pound All-State fullback, out weighed the average Heart Mountain lineman by sixty pounds. [12]

Casper fullback Leroy Pierce carrying the ball in the Heart Mountain Eagles' only defeat (YHC).

In addition to the new high school, 1943 brought a number of other changes to Heart Mountain's school system. In July, high school principle John Corbett took over as superintendent when C. D. Carter left to join the service. It was during that school year that Tommy Main became the first Caucasian student in the Heart Mountain school system. In mid October Victor Ryan enrolled his nine-year-old daughter in school at the camp, and she became the second Caucasian student in the center. Both the Main and Ryan families were employed at Heart Mountain. It was fortunate for some Japanese American students that Tommy Main was attending school in the camp. Since he was Caucasian, Main could come and go as he pleased, and on occasion he invited friends to attend the movies with him in Cody. In some instances, it was the first time that the Japanese American students had been outside the camp since their arrival a year and one-half earlier. [13]

At Heart Mountain, students and teachers got along very well for the most part. As in any other schools, there were teachers students liked and others they did not care for. Both students and teachers had to make adjustments. Most teachers had never had any prior contact with students of Japanese ancestry and certainly not in the numbers they had at Heart Mountain. Clarissa Corbett, who taught home economics at the high school, said she had some prejudices when she first arrived at camp, but found that the color of ones skin had nothing to do with what was inside. Corbett enjoyed her teaching experience at Heart Mountain. Irene Damme taught for two years at Heart Mountain and said, " . . . everything has run very smoothly for me here and I have enjoyed it more than public school work." Looking back, Barbara (Miller) Nyden, who taught only three months at Heart Mountain, during the spring of 1945, said of her teaching experience, "I liked my students, but, in truth, I did not enjoy it." [14]

Most students remember school as being the central focus of their lives at Heart Mountain. Prior to evacuation, many of them attended schools where the student body was predominantly Caucasian. In camp, they had to adjust to being in all Japanese American classes. Ike Hatchimonji said that after settling into a routine, school was about the same in camp as it had been on the outside. One of the first problems encountered was with Caucasian instructors trying to pronounce Japanese names. Ike's twin brother Mike said some teachers compounded the problem by trying to make Japanese names out of students' American names. Mike said one teacher pronounced his name "me-kay" and his brother's "i-kay." That instructor was under the impression that everyone with a Japanese face had a Japanese name. Simple problems of this nature were quickly remedied, but they added to the time involved in the already difficult getting-acquainted process between student and teacher. [15]

According to one Heart Mountain student, the only real problem he had in school was trying to avoid members of certain clubs, particularly the "Taiyos" and the "Exclusive 20." These clubs, or gangs, were made up of older boys, many out of school, who enjoyed picking on and terrorizing some of the younger children. The children in camp did not have the chores or responsibilities they had at home. And with poor lighting and crowded living conditions in the barracks apartments, homework from school was at times discouraged by the school administration. This, along with the fact that some parents did not see their teenaged children from the time they departed for school in the morning until they returned home for bed, left some students with too much time on their hands. That, in turn, led to cases of juvenile delinquency. [16]

Once a settled routine was established, teachers and teaching assistants worked fairly well together, and each appreciated the efforts the other put into the classes. Bea Araki, who had majored in education and home economics in college, was made teaching assistant to Lois Kurtz. Mrs. Kurtz taught home economics for grades nine and twelve while Clarissa Corbett taught the same courses to sophomores and juniors. Corbett said that the first year of school was mostly book work since no sewing machines, cooking supplies or equipment was available. After they moved into the new high school, old sewing machines were picked up through donations made by people on the outside. Corbett said she was impressed with the work turned out by her students. Araki, along with other assistants and the students, was very appreciative of Kurtz and Corbett, who would often make a trip to Powell or Cody when supplies were low to purchase material and other sewing equipment with their own money. Araki described the two teachers as, "super people." [17]

Kaoru Inouye, who became a teaching assistant and teacher, graduated

Home Economics class (ERC).

from the University of California at Berkeley in 1938 with a degree in chemistry. Inouye was working for Hooper Research Labratory at the University of California Medical Center when he was evacuated to the Santa Anita Assembly Center. At Heart Mountain, Inouye was responsible for teaching physics and chemistry in the camp's high school. The students and the teacher were both challenged that first year in a chemistry class that depended on experiments which could be devised from whatever Inouye dug up in the mess hall for equipment and chemicals. [18] The situation improved the second year as the new high school was equipped with a chemistry lab and all the equipment required for proper instruction and experiments.

Inouye was also active in other areas within the school. He taught adult education classes in the evenings, as did other instructors, and worked at high school activities such as dances and sporting events. In addition, Inouye served on the Board of Trustees for Community Activities and played an important role in determining the design of the Heart Mountain High School diploma. He felt that the experiences already faced by students had been difficult enough, and Inouye did not want the students to receive diplomas which indicated, in any way, that they were issued within the confines of a concentration camp. The WRA wanted the diplomas signed by the project director. However, through Inouye's lobbying, the only signatures to appear on the Heart Mountain High School diploma were those of the principal and superintendent. [19]

Inouye's work did not go unnoticed or unappreciated. Even though he was paid only $19 per month, he went far beyond what was expected of him. The school superintendent at Heart Mountain said Inouye spent many hours with the senior class working on the commencement program and was also invaluable in the maintenance and repair of science equipment in the high school. His technical knowledge was also an asset. Before the first basketball game with a team from the outside, the coach had refinished the floor in the gym and painted new boundary lines. A problem arose when the start of the game was drawing near and the paint was still wet. Inouye applied lampblack to the paint and it dried within minutes. The game was played on schedule. [20]

With the devotion of internees like Kaoru Inouye and Bea Araki who worked long hours for the benefit of the students, despite their meager salaries, and the selfless efforts of Caucasian teachers like Lois Kurtz and Clarissa Corbett, who sometimes purchased school supplies with their own money, Heart Mountain was able to function, for the most part, as a normal school system. However, in spite of outward appearances, there were a number of underlying problems which teachers and administrators faced daily.

Not only did Carter and Corbett face the problem of setting up a school system for a community with a population exceeding 10,000, but they also had to do so under the watchful eye and policies of the project director and director of the WRA. Although project director Chris Rachford, and later, Guy Robertson, seldom interfered in the hiring process, the director gave final approval for the hiring of all government employees at Heart Mountain, including teachers. Decisions of that sort would have been better left to the educators who established the minimum education requirements and standards for teachers in the camp. [21]

The first head of the WRA's Education Section was Lucy W. Adams, who had recently served as director for the Navajo Reservation's school system. Adams established policies at the WRA which mirrored those used at schools on the reservation. The idea was to teach the skills necessary to live in American society. Since it was believed that one reason the Japanese had been evacuated was due their cultural ties to Japan, instruction in American democracy was of primary importance. The problems were obvious. How did one teach the tenets of democracy to an incarcerated student body? While reciting the "Pledge of Allegiance," a student could be saying the lines, "One nation, under God, indivisible, with liberty and justice to all" at the same time he or she was looking out a window at guard towers and a barbed wire fence. [22]

The school superintendent at the Minidoka Relocation Center in Idaho saw no problems with teaching democracy to incarcerated students. He said that the evacuation experience would help the Japanese to realize the advantages of living in a democratic country once they were allowed to leave the camps. At Heart Mountain, student body president, Ted Fujioka, worked to acquire the flag pole from an abandoned CCC camp in Powell. The flag pole was moved to the camp high school, and a date for a formal ceremony was set for the raising of the colors. Principal Corbett was not excited about the ceremony and told Fujioka that many of the students might not want to salute the flag. Fujioka explained to Corbett that there was "nothing to worry about." On December 22, 1942, the Boy Scout Drum and Bugle Corps played *To the Colors* as the student body saluted during the flag raising ceremony. [23]

The study of democracy within the confines of a concentration camp had so disillusioned high school students that some decided not to attend college. A survey of seniors at a camp in Arkansas revealed that prior to evacuation nearly forty-six percent of the students planned to go on to college. After evacuation, only fourteen percent said they intended to continue their education. In addition, the WRA was pushing high school graduates into accepting vocational training instead of a college education. The WRA believed that such training would be of more immediate help in the war effort. An independent educational consultant believed that such a policy was detrimental to the students and did not prepare them for life in post-war American society. [24]

In 1943 and 1944, twenty states had adopted various laws authorizing prohibitive actions against Japanese and Japanese Americans. At Amache, the relocation center in Colorado, the camp parent-teacher association tried to join the state PTA organization and was refused recognition. Discriminatory laws and the biases of outside organizations were destroying the lessons instructors at Heart Mountain and other camps were teaching on American democracy. It became safer for internees to stay in camp as opposed to relocating. In 1944, the Supreme Court, in *Ex Parte Endo*, ruled that it was illegal for the government to hold loyal American citizens against their will. It was apparent that the camps would close by the end of the war. This combination of events, anti-Japanese sentiment which caused internees to remain in camp, and the Endo decision which allowed evacuees to return to the West Coast, forced the WRA to take a different tack as far as its education policy was concerned. The WRA wanted teachers to begin emphasizing the importance of relocating. It was hoped that the children would have some influence on their parents and grandparents in that matter. [25]

In spite of trying to teach a curriculum which was constantly influenced by changing WRA policy, teachers and students at Heart Mountain persevered. Teachers taught and students learned. The Heart Mountain school system did not encounter the massive student walkouts, or parents holding their children out of school, which took place at Topaz in Utah and Tule Lake in California. [26]

While school kept the younger people busy most of the time, something else was needed to occupy their free time. Adults who worked also need some sort of relaxation and recreation. In addition, there were also large numbers of older people who had nothing to do but sit in their rooms. Since the residents could not leave camp and go into Powell or Cody without a special pass, other activities had to be found within the center.

Chapter VIII

Camp Activities

Boredom was one of the biggest problems internees faced at Heart Mountain. The very young and the older residents who could not work or attend school had to have some sorts of activities to keep them busy. Without something to occupy their time, internees would sit and think about all they had lost and the situation in which they found themselves. Even those who worked or attended school required some form of recreation. As soon as the camp was occupied, the administration appointed a Camp Activities Supervisor. The supervisor, Marlin Kurtz, was responsible for organizing and scheduling activities for what would be nearly 11,000 people. [1]

The activities supervisor was responsible for seven different departments. The camp's Scheduling Department coordinated and scheduled all special activities and regular activities that took place in the mess halls, recreation halls and the high school gym. The job of scheduling was complex and became more so with the increase in different types of activities available to residents until 1945, when, due to relocation and preparations for closing the camp, activities were scaled back. [2]

Before the two movie theaters, the "Dawn" and the "Pagoda," were established, movies were scheduled and shown in the mess halls. They were scheduled so that, when the first reel of the film ended in one mess hall, it was rushed to another building where it was started for a different audience. In the meantime the previous mess hall began showing reel number two. The first film shown in camp, "Freckles Comes Home," debuted on Saturday, October 24, for the residents of Blocks one and two. Movies were the most popular form of entertainment in the camp. From October 1942 through September 1945, attendance at film presentations was 600,908. The movies during that period took in $48,072.70. The price of admission was ten cents for adults and five cents for children. Youngsters under the age of six were admitted free. [3]

The department was also responsible for scheduling non-recreation activities such as church services. The Protestant denominations established a Community Christian Church which was made up of a number of groups; Salvation Army, Presbyterian, Methodist, Baptist, Union, Reform Christian and Seventh Day Adventist. While a few denominations held their own services, the majority combined to hold joint services which took place in the recreation hall in Block 22, which had been remodeled as a church with equipment donated by various outside church groups. For example, Reverend A. J. Kammon of the Cody Presbyterian Church made a loan to the camp's Christian Church of a pulpit and organ. Women from the Catholic church and the five Protestant churches in Powell organized the "Christian Good Will Group." Those women collected and donated clothes to the camp and often met with the Christian women's group from Heart Mountain. [4]

The Protestant ministers of Powell and Cody also had a group that visited the ministers at Heart Mountain on a twice-monthly basis. Other activities within the Community Christian Church included choir and Chi Sigma Lambda, a boys and girls club which, according to Mike Hatchimonji, sponsored parties, dances and even a box social. Hatchimonji said he could never figure out where the girls got the food to make box lunches for the social. The churches also supplied other forms of diversion for some residents. One of Bea Araki's favorite pastimes was singing in the church choir and teaching Sunday School. [5]

In addition to the Community Christian Church, there was one Catholic Church. The Catholics in camp numbered only around 100, but they had their own church which was ministered by Father Felsecher, a Maryknoll priest who had lived in Japan for ten years. Felsecher lived in Powell with Father Kimmet, but his sole purpose for coming to the area was to serve the Catholic population of Heart Mountain. When he first arrived at Heart Mountain, Father Felsecher tried to establish a residence at the camp, but the WRA would not allow it. On one occasion, Father Lavery, from Los Angeles, made a trip to Heart Mountain for the sole purpose of visiting his former parishioners. [6]

The Reverend Herbert Nicholson (seated center) made a trip to Heart Mountain to visit friends and members of his congregation (JTIC).

Besides the Christians, the WRA estimated that two thirds of those who claimed an attachment to any religion were Buddhists. There were eight Buddhist priests among the camp's population and a short time after the center opened, there were five different Buddhist churches. In an effort to make better use of the existing facilities, and in the interest of easier scheduling, the administration suggested that the Buddhists organize on the same principle as the Protestants. That was done in November 1942, and a single Buddhist congregation was formed. Three of the eight priests appealed to the camp's administration for the right to start their own church, but were turned down. Since the internees' civil rights had all ready been blatantly abused, the administration showed little concern with "Freedom of Religion." Nevertheless, the problem was solved when, in the fall of 1943, two of the three priests wanting to form their own church were labeled as trouble makers and banished to the segregation center at Tule Lake, California. One of the priests was eventually repatriated to Japan.[7]

Along with the Sunday services and functions sponsored by the various church groups, there were a good many other activities within the camp. The Activities Section, in cooperation with the Engineering Section, graded off a number softball fields. Softball and baseball were the most popular summertime activities. Mori Shimada said the older residents would pack the stands for baseball and softball games. There were softball leagues for the different age groups and for boys and girls. Participation was extensive.[8]

One of several Heart Mountain baseball teams (YHC).

Another summer activity was swimming. During the summer of 1943, a large pit was excavated and lined with gravel. The pit became the camp swimming pool. It was constructed just below the irrigation canal that ran through the project so there would be easy access to water with which to keep the pool filled. In 1944 a chlorinator was installed to comply with Wyoming state regulations. The pool was open from 9:00 a.m. to 9:00 p.m. and was supplied with a lifeguard and swimming instructors. The Boy Scouts used the pool for their swimming tests and for lifesaving practice. [9]

Young girls enjoying a summer day at the pool (ERC).

During the winter months there was judo, boxing, basketball, volleyball, badminton and weight lifting. The most popular outdoor sport in the wintertime was ice skating. That first winter, 1942\43, the fire department flooded the large open area where the new high school was later built and allowed it to freeze. In following years a small dike was built around the football field, and when it was flooded, it became the main skating rink. There were also a number of smaller rinks as fire hydrants on most blocks were opened on occasion and allowed to flood a small area. Arthur Tsuneishi said that Sears and Roebuck was popular even in the winter months as internees ordered not only winter clothing, but a large number of ice skates. Many of those who had never seen snow before being sent to Heart Mountain became proficient ice skaters. [10]

Ice skating at Heart Mountain (ERC).

Another popular sport with the children during the winter months was sledding. A number of fathers built sleds out of scrap lumber for their children. The sledding, however, did not last long that first winter. Early in November 1942, thirty-two boys varying in age from seven to eleven, were arrested and hauled to the guardhouse by MP's for sledding outside the confines of the camp. The barbed wire fence was not constructed around the camp until late November and early December of 1942, but the young boys were sledding about fifty yards beyond where the fence was going to be built. They were arrested, taken in, and their sleds confiscated. The mother of an eight year old was at a loss for an explanation when her son asked what bad thing he had done to be taken to jail. In the months that followed, however, such restrictions were relaxed. Moving through the front gate

71

required a pass, so internees would simply climb through the barbed wire fence surrounding the camp and freely roam the area from the Shoshone River to the top of Heart Mountain itself. [11]

Heart Mountain Boy Scout (ERC).

One of the most popular activities for both boys and girls was scouting. Scouting not only provided an outlet for pent-up energy, but it also made for stiff competition between different scout troops. The competition helped develop a pride in each troop and the individuals within the troops. Raymond Uno belonged to troop 145, which consisted mainly of boys from the Maryknoll Catholic school in Los Angeles. Troop 145's chief competitor was Troop 379, also from Los Angeles. Troop 379 was one of the top troops in the nation. There were also Troops 35, 145 and Troop 38 from the San Jose area. The boys swam, hiked and camped on the banks of the Shoshone River below the camp. [12]

Mike Hatchimonji was a member of Troop 345 and also the Boy Scout's Drum and Bugle Corps. He said they invited the Scouts from Cody to the camp and worked out a sort of friendly competition between the two. It turned out to be the city boys against the country boys. Pete Simpson of Cody remembered the first Heart Mountain jamboree which Cody's Troop 250 attended. The Scoutmasters from both Cody and Heart Mountain addressed the gathering in patriotic terms and spoke of preparing for life and the future. The boys from Cody seemed impressed with the fact that the Heart Mountain Scouts spoke perfect English. Following the formal address, the boys worked on merit badges. Simpson was paired with a Scout from Troop 379. Though the day was quite enjoyable, it was also embarrassing. Simpson was a native of the "Cowboy State," which in his mind suggested an ability to use a rope. While working on merit badges, Simpson had trouble tying a single knot; however, his partner, a city boy from Troop 379, could tie knots with his eyes closed. [13] Over the years of the camp's existence there were a number of interactions between Scouting groups from Powell, Cody and Heart Mountain.

According to Mike Hatchimonji, the Boy Scout Drum and Bugle Corps was an extension of Troop 379, but anyone in Scouting could join. He was not quite sure where the Corps got its instruments, but there seemed to be enough for all the members. Toyoo Nitake said that on the 4th of July, the Boy Scouts and Girl Scouts would parade between the barracks with the Drum and Bugle Corps in a celebration of American independence. During those parades, Nitake said, "Something seemed good [sic] yet something seemed wrong." [14]

Heart Mountain's Girl Scout Leaders (ERC).

Scouting was also an important part of life for the girls at Heart Mountain. Yas Ikeda said the Girl Scouts worked for badges and held camp-wide gatherings. While the boys had a Drum and Bugle Corps, the girls had a drill team. Like the boys, the Girl Scouts also went camping along the banks of the Shoshone River on occasion. Ikeda did not grow up in a Japanese American community, so scouting also gave her the opportunity to learn more about her Japanese heritage. On camp outs the girls discussed life at Heart Mountain and life before evacuation. In those exchanges, Ikeda learned a great deal about Japanese culture. Jean Ushijima said her Scout group was able to make a trip to Cody to visit the Buffalo Bill Museum which they enjoyed immensely. The down side of the trip, and perhaps the most memorable part, was the number of signs the girls saw in store windows which read, "No Japs." As with the boys, Girl Scout troops from nearby Powell and Cody traveled to Heart Mountain on a number of occasions and participated in numerous activities. [15]

For the most part, the camping and hiking activities of the Scouts were restricted to the Shoshone River area and the hills around Heart Mountain. However, social workers who visited the camp said that the environment in the center was having an adverse effect on the children. In an effort to counter that, arrangements were made for the Boy Scouts and Girl Scouts to spend a week camping in Yellowstone Park. The CCC camp in the park was scheduled to be dismantled late in the summer of 1944. Earlier that summer, the 500 Scouts from Heart Mountain were sent in groups of 100 to Yellowstone where they were able to spend one week hiking and camping while using the facilities of the CCC camp. [16]

Kabuki theater performer (ERC).

Activities

There were a great many activities for the adults, with participation estimated at 6,000 individuals per week. The Scheduling Department listed twenty-seven official activities with forty-two instructors. There were sewing and knitting classes, wood carving, and many others. The residents also engaged in a number of traditional Japanese activities. However, it was the policy of the administration to discourage Japanese cultural activities in favor of more "American" pursuits. No type of Japanese entertainment was sponsored by the administration, but it was permitted. Activities such as Kabuki, one type of Japanese theater, or the Bon Odori festival, the annual Japanese festival of the dead, were previewed by camp officials before permits were issued for the events. [17]

Internees also participated in other Japanese cultural activities. Two places were set aside for the playing of Japanese games of goh and shogi. Lessons were given for the biwa, a Japanese instrument similar to the lute, and in calligraphy, the writing of Japanese and Chinese characters with ink and brush. Many internees pursued their own interests. Arthur Tsuneishi's father was a well known haiku poet and established a haiku club. He also started a Japanese library and spent many hours translating English classics into Japanese. Other internees organized clubs which dealt with Japanese cultural activities such as flower arranging and bonsai classes. [18]

Flower arranging competition (ERC).

75

The most popular of the Japanese cultural activities was the annual Bon Odori festival in which the participants would dance the traditional folk dances in a big circle. The festival was held in a large open area of the camp. Kabuki theater was the other popular type of cultural entertainment. Performances were usually given every two months. The troop consisted of between fifty and sixty performers and assistants. On average, each show drew 400 to 500 spectators with a number of performances being given in the various blocks. [19]

The administration sponsored ping pong tournaments, chess, checkers, and card games. Bridge clubs were quite popular. George Igawa organized a camp orchestra which played for numerous dances within the camp. There was also another musical group known as the "Hawaiian Surf Riders" who were popular not only in camp, but throughout the Big Horn Basin. The "Surf Riders" made numerous appearances on the local radio station in Powell. Both the camp orchestra and the Surf Riders played at dances in Powell, Lovell, Cowley and Cody. [20]

Letter writing was another of the more popular activities in camp. It not only helped pass the time, it also allowed internees to find out what was going on back home. Writing about the difficulties faced in camp was a way of getting things off one's chest and blowing off steam. An average of 3,500 pieces of mail left the camp every day. The internees were spending nearly $100 per day on stamps. Many letters were to family members in the army who were serving their country and fighting for the democracy that had locked their families behind barbed wire. [21]

Some evacuees collected rocks on the expanse of the project. There were also a great number of shells to be found in the area since it had once been under water. The shells were made into pins and other pieces of jewelry. Victory Gardens were a popular pastime. About eight acres of land on the west side of the camp were set aside and divided into 20x40 foot plots. Approximately 145 families maintained Victory Gardens. Some residents, who wanted an occasional drink, made rice wine. Frank Hayami's neighbor got drunk one day on a concoction he made by fermenting raisins, an activity not endorsed by the WRA. Hayami could never figure out where the raisins came from. [22]

Some internees put their names on waiting lists in the hope of obtaining a pass to leave camp and visit Powell, Cody or Billings, Montana. Most residents were very fortunate to travel to one of the towns just once during the time they spent at Heart Mountain. For young mothers like Ada Endo and Emi Kuromiya, the only activity other than child care was an occasional game of cards with the neighbors. [23]

Even though there were a great many different activities to occupy internees, in addition to work and school, boredom was still a major problem. Many evacuees did the same thing day after day for more than three years. A continual problem faced by the administration was keeping qualified people to run the camp's activity programs. The younger internees were usually trying to relocate and get out of the camp. As early as April 1943, one of the Scout troops had to be disbanded when the Scout leader relocated and a qualified replacement could not be found. [24] While relocation offered those who left, freedom and the opportunity to start over, it often compounded the problems of those left behind.

Chapter IX

Relocation

The WRA's Relocation Division at Heart Mountain was established on August 10, 1942, two days before the official opening of the camp. The first duty of the division was to register the internees and then find housing and jobs for them as they entered the center. After the evacuees had arrived, the responsibilities of the division changed. The next priority was to help internees make plans for finding permanent or temporary employment outside the camp. [1]

The relocation program was set up with three different types of leave available to residents. Short-term leave permitted evacuees to travel to areas outside the camp in order to check relocation possibilities and job prospects. Indefinite leave allowed the evacuees to work and live in communities east of the Mississippi River on a trial basis. A short time later, that was changed to include certain areas west of the Mississippi. Seasonal leave gave Heart Mountain residents the opportunity to work outside the camp, usually on agricultural projects, and then return when the work was completed. The WRA decided later that seasonal leave did little to promote the idea of relocation and only served to help area farmers harvest their crops. The WRA felt that those on seasonal passes were only out to make enough money so that they could return to camp and live in economic comfort through the winter. The seasonal program was ended early in 1945 with only terminal work leaves being granted. [2]

Early attempts by internees to relocate were caught up in a "bottle neck." The procedures were typical of most government operations. First the individual had to make an application for leave. The application was submitted to the relocation office in camp, which sent it to the regional office in Denver. It was then passed on to Washington. After reviewing each case individually, Washington would notify Denver, which in turn notified Heart Mountain, with officials there eventually getting back to the individual who applied. Even though that process was eventually abandoned and requests were sent directly to Washington, problems still existed. An internee could only receive a leave clearance after his or her case was evaluated by a board made up of representatives of the WRA, the army and the navy. Some received permanent leave to any location in the East or Midwest, while others were allowed leave as long as they stayed out of areas under the Eastern Defense Command. A few residents had their names added to permanent "stop lists" and were not allowed leave of any type. [3]

If internees were fortunate enough to receive a leave permit, it was then up to them to complete all of the paper work involved on their own. The family, or individual, had to make arrangements to ship personal property, apply for any clothing allowance or wages he or she might be owed, and get a release which stated that any government property issued to the individual had been returned. The internee then had to purchase tickets for transportation, pick up any relocation grant money that may have been due, and make arrangements to get to bus or train depots for departure. It was 1944 before the division began to help the internee through this process. A frightening aspect of the process came in a statement made by Joe Carroll (head of the camp's Relocation Division) in his final report. Carroll said, "should there ever again be need for the handling of a group of people [in such a manner], . . . It would be better that . . . existing government agencies be utilized . . . to secure control of the problem much easier and much sooner." [4] Carroll was already looking ahead to the next time that the government might choose to evacuate some of its citizens.

The Relocation Division organized a group of internees into a Relocation Committee. That group did more work toward the relocation of the residents of Heart Mountain than government officials in the camp. The Relocation Committee, with the help of the American Friends Service and the YMCA, provided information on the availability of jobs on the outside. The American Friends Service, along with other church organizations, did a great deal of work assisting the internees. Even with the help of outside groups, relocation was still a problem. Although locations west of the Mississippi had been opened up to internee resettlement, the WRA put quotas on those areas. In many instances, an internee or family member might have found a job, in Salt Lake City for example, but due to the quota system they were not allowed to settle there because Salt Lake City was said to be at the "saturation point." In other words, the quota of Japanese allowed to live in that city was already filled. The individual or family was forced to look elsewhere. [5]

WRA officials believed that many of the problems faced by the internees, and one of the principle reasons for their evacuation, was the fact that they moved into ethnic enclaves or, Japantowns. The WRA encouraged those relocating from the camps to disperse throughout the country. Internees were even discouraged from meeting and appearing in public in groups. This policy was, to some extent, successful, as by the time the last camp closed, nearly one-third of the previously incarcerated population lived outside the West Coast area. Since the vast majority of those relocating were college-educated Nisei from nonagricultural backgrounds, most fitted easily back into American society outside the West Coast. [6] But their experiences varied. Some moved to areas where they were warmly and immediately accepted and their contributions to society appreciated; others were taken advantage of or could not find decent jobs.

Bill Hosokawa, editor of the *Heart Mountain Sentinel*, began making preparations to leave camp early in the summer of 1943. However, as was the case with most individuals trying to relocate, finding a job on the outside proved easier than getting out of camp. Hosokawa was hired as a copyeditor by the *Des Moines Register* in Iowa. When he and his family finally received permission to leave, they were given twenty-five dollars each (a relocation allotment) and escorted to the front gate where they boarded a bus bound for Billings, Montana. In Billings, the Hosokawas boarded a train bound for, ironically, Independence, Missouri.[7]

Upon arriving in Missouri, Hosokawa left his family with his brother, who lived in Kansas City, while he traveled on to Des Moines to look for a place to live. Like many others, he stayed at a hostel run by the Quakers. Hosokawa reported for work and looked for a house to rent in his spare time. He soon found a two-story house and sent for his family. Though glad to be out of the camp, Hosokawa said the wind whistled through the house in Des Moines all winter. At times "it was like being back at Heart Mountain, . . ." The Hosokawas remained in Des Moines until 1946 when they moved to Denver.[8]

While at Heart Mountain, Ruth Hashimoto received a telegram in June of 1943 asking if she would consider working as an instructor at the Naval Intelligence Language School in Boulder, Colorado. Since Hashimoto had taken a Japanese language test earlier in the year, Naval Intelligence was aware of her abilities. Hashimoto's husband opposed the idea of his wife working for the federal government. He told her, "Uncle Sam put us here. We're going to stay here until he takes us back home again."[9] Three months later, approximately one dozen individuals who had taken the Japanese language test were called from Heart Mountain to Denver. The prospective instructors were interviewed by Dr. Joseph Yamagiwa from the University of Michigan. Yamagiwa was in search of instructors willing to work at the Japanese Language School located at Ann Arbor, Michigan. Hashimoto wanted to raise her children outside the barbed wire confines of Heart Mountain, so when offered the job, she accepted.[10]

Hashimoto's husband was against her leaving Heart Mountain and threatened her if she should try to depart. He told her that when Japan won the war she would be put up against a wall and shot (Mr. Hashimoto was an Issei and his wife a Nisei). Fearing for her safety, Hashimoto was escorted out of camp to the train depot by the Military Police. She left her two daughters with a brother in Peoria, Illinois, while she traveled on to Ann Arbor to report for work and locate a place to live. Mr. Sakai, who was living in Ann Arbor and had also been interned at Heart Mountain, told Hashimoto that she and her children could live with his family until they found a place of their own.[11]

When Hashimoto arrived in Ann Arbor with her children Sakai was nowhere to be found. When she telephoned his house, Hashimoto was informed by Mrs. Sakai, that she did not want to be bothered with them. Hashimoto shared a room in a private home with another instructor and slept on the floor while her daughters slept in the twin size bed. That temporarily solved the problem of sleeping arrangements, but Hashimoto still had to find a day-care to look after the children while she taught classes. She found a woman who would care for the children if Hashimoto would come during her lunch break to help feed the other babies the woman cared for and return again after work to clean the house. In addition, she was required to pay the woman $100 a month. Hashimoto was only paid $200 a month. [12]

After two months in that situation, Hashimoto's students discovered what she was going through and went out on their own time and found their instructor an

apartment and a day-care, which charged only $28 per month. While one person took advantage of her desperate situation, others whom she barely knew came to her aid. [13]

Frank Hayami was allowed to relocate from Heart Mountain in August of 1943. He left camp with one suitcase and $100 in his pocket, and headed for New York. Even though he possessed a degree in electrical engineering, the best job Hayami could find was bussing tables in restaurants. His draft card designation of 4-C (enemy alien) did not help him when looking for an engineering job. How an American citizen could be designated as an alien, enemy or otherwise, was a problem that

Yoshio Yoshida relocated to Des Moines, Iowa where he worked as a cook (ERC).

Japanese Americans contemplated throughout the war and for years after. [14]

Mary Oyama Mittwer, a very talented writer, relocated with her family to Denver in late January 1943. Even though she was in camp only a short time, she made a significant contribution to the understanding of camp life through her column in the *Powell Tribune*, "Heart Mountain Breezes" (Oyama's work, which resulted in the cordial relationship between the residents of Powell and Heart Mountain will be reviewed in a later chapter). [15]

The relocation process also resulted in a number of families being split apart. Arthur Tsuneishi relocated to Chicago in 1943 where he found a job as a dishwasher. However, in 1944 Tsuneishi had a spinal operation and was told that in order to recover properly he should move to a warmer climate. With this in mind, Tsuneishi resettled at the Poston Relocation Center in Arizona where he was joined by his mother, who left Heart Mountain to care for him. Florence Tsuneishi, a sister, relocated to Minnesota where she taught Japanese to army personnel. Another sister, Frances, was caught in Japan when the war broke out. Two brothers were serving with the army in the South Pacific, while a third brother attended the University of Wyoming. Tsuneishi's younger sister, Rose, and his father, remained at Heart Mountain until 1945 when the government began closing down the camp. [16] The government's policy of forced removal of all people of Japanese ancestry from the West Coast resulted in the Tsuneishi family, and many others, being torn apart and scattered across the United States.

Toshiko (Nagamori) Ito (second from the right) on vacation in Yellowstone Park, 1939 (JTIC).

Like Noel Tsuneishi, who left camp to attend college at the University of Wyoming, a number of other young people also left Heart Mountain to enroll in school. Most relocated and attended colleges in the East or Midwest. Prospective students had an easier time relocating if they had someone on the outside to assist them. Toshiko (Nagamori) Ito had some acquaintances in Missouri who helped her get into National College in Kansas City. Even with outside help, the process was slow. Ito could not believe the amount of work involved just to apply for a student leave. She complained to her mother that a man in the student relocation office made her fill out what seemed to be miles of forms in triplicate (she later married the guy, James Ito). By the time her leave was approved and Ito arrived at college, classes had already been in session for six weeks. [17] Many of those who were able to relocate to attend school that first year arrived in camp late and had to wait until the spring semester began.

As in the case of Arthur Tsuneishi, an internee with good reason could apply to move to another relocation center. Eugene Sasai was raised by his grandparents, and when evacuation came, they were all sent to the Topaz Relocation Center in Utah. Shortly after arriving at Topaz, Sasai's grandfather died. In 1944 Sasai's grandmother applied for and received permission to relocate to Heart Mountain. She had made plans to marry a man who was interned there. When he arrived, Sasai said that compared to Topaz, Heart Mountain was a "beehive of energy." [18]

Eugene Sasai went from one relocation center to another under good conditions. Miyoko (Takeuchi) Eshita went from a relocation center to an internment camp under very tragic circumstances. Eshita's father, who was a gardener, had been picked up by the FBI in March of 1942. He was placed in internment camps (administered by the Justice Department) at Santa Fe and Lordsburg, New Mexico. The interment camps were much smaller than relocation centers and housed individuals who the government felt were a possible threat to national security (those placed in these camps were given hearings and some won their release). Most of the people incarcerated in those camps were placed there because they were community leaders, or because they subscribed to certain publications which it was believed were influenced by the Japanese Government. [19]

Eshita, her mother, brother, and three sisters were sent to Heart Mountain from the Pomona Assembly Center. With her father incarcerated in New Mexico, Eshita's family looked to her uncle Genichiro Nishiyama as the head of the household. On November 10, 1942, Nishiyama was helping to dismantle a nearby CCC camp which was to be reconstructed at Heart Mountain. During the job he fell ten feet from a scaffold and was killed. After hearing of the accident, Eshita's father applied for a transfer to the family internment camp at Crystal City, Texas. If an individual in an internment camp had a family in a relocation center and they wished to join him, they could, with approval, all relocate to the family internment camp. In June of 1943, after she received her high school diploma at Heart Mountain, Eshita and her family relocated to Crystal City, and joined their father. [20]

A small number of internees who made their way to Heart Mountain were Japanese Nationals who were visiting the United States when the war broke out and were caught in this country. There were approximately 1,500 Japanese Nationals in that situation throughout the United States who applied for repatriation and were accepted by the Japanese government. They were to be exchanged for Westerners interned in Japan under similar circumstances. On August 29, 1943, thirty-three residents of Heart Mountain, who were Japanese citizens, departed by train for

Jersey City, New Jersey. There they boarded the Swedish ship, Gripsholm, and sailed to Goa, a Portuguese colony in India where the exchanges took place. [21]

Another much larger group of Heart Mountaineers was relocated to Tule Lake, California. Tule Lake, at one time, was a relocation center much like the one at Heart Mountain. In July of 1943, following a meeting of relocation center representatives held in Denver, WRA officials said they had a need to convert one of the ten camps into a segregation center. There they would house the "trouble makers" and those who asked to be repatriated to Japan. An internee could also be sent to Tule Lake if he or she applied for, and failed to receive, a leave clearance. [22]

The necessity for a segregation camp came about when Secretary of War Henry Stimson was considering the possibility of an all Nisei army unit which would fight in Europe. In order to put together such a unit it became necessary for the government to find out which Japanese Americans were loyal to the United States. The government had all Issei and Nisei over the age of seventeen fill out a "loyalty questionnaire." The answers determined, at least in the eyes of the government, who was loyal and who was not. A great deal of trouble and controversy arose over the phrasing of two of the questions in particular, questions twenty-seven and twenty-eight. [23]

Question twenty-seven was aimed toward those Nisei who could be drafted or allowed to volunteer for military service. The question, however, was also given to women and the Issei, and caused much confusion. The two questions read as follows:

27. Are you willing to serve in the armed forces of the United States on combat duty, wherever ordered?

28. Will you swear unqualified allegiance to the United States of America and faithfully defend the United States from any or all attack by foreign or domestic forces, and foreswear any form of allegiance or obedience to the Japanese emperor, to any other foreign government, power or organization? [24]

The problem with these questions was not only the phrasing, but also the fact that only a Yes or No answer was allowed, though many did qualify their answers. The women and the very old had no desire or intention to serve in combat duty. Therefore some answered "No" to question twenty-seven. Question twenty-eight caused problems for all who answered it, even though only about 5% replied "No." Asking the Nisei to foreswear allegiance to the emperor of Japan was seen by most as an insult. They were American citizens and had never known any country but the United States. The question was then asking the Issei to leave themselves without a country. Japan, which many of the Issei had not seen for thirty to fifty years, had done nothing to them. The United States, on the other hand, which was their home, had locked them behind barbed wire and would not allow them become citizens. If one answered "Yes" to the question, he or she was admitting some sort of loyalty to the emperor of Japan. If the answer was "No," the individual was seen as a traitor in the eyes of the United States Government. Frank Hayami said that answering question twenty-eight was equivalent to responding to the question, "Have you stopped beating your wife?" No matter what the answer, some sort guilt was inferred. [25]

To answer "No" to either question, no matter what the reason, suggested disloyalty as far as the WRA and the federal government were concerned. The questionnaire figured prominently in the "Draft Resister's Trial" (which will be discussed later) and in the relocation plans of some individuals. Those answering "No" to either question twenty-seven or twenty-eight, or both, and those upset with the government for even asking such questions, some of whom asked to be repatriated to Japan, were sent to the segregation center at Tule Lake. Those at Tule Lake who answered "Yes" to both questions were transferred to one of the nine other relocation centers. On September 18, 1943, 431 "loyal" internees left Tule Lake for Heart Mountain. When the train arrived, 432 "disloyal" internees, approximately three percent of the camp's population, from Heart Mountain made the return trip to Tule Lake. In all, nearly 900 Heart Mountain residents made the move to Tule Lake with about the same number of Tule Lake internees being sent to Heart Mountain. [26]

The parents of Joyce Mori decided that they wanted to stay in the United States no matter what happened. Even though they did not appreciate the loyalty questionnaire, they gave affirmative answers to the questions. However, over a period of time, Mori's father changed his mind. After spending long hours conversing with friends and neighbors, he decided to ask for repatriation and move his family back to Japan. He did not inform his wife and children of his decision until it was time to pack for the journey. When he did finally tell them of the plans he had made, Mori said that the family fought like never before. But in the end, they made the trip together. They were first relocated to Tule Lake and then to Japan. [27]

Mori said her family boarded a boat and sailed for Japan in December of 1945. The war was over, but since her father had applied for repatriation, the family was sent to Japan. Mori said that the day the boat left was the most unbearable and devastating she had ever faced. It was difficult to control the tears. Even today she is not sure whether her mother ever forgave her father for listening to friends and neighbors instead of discussing the matter with the family. Mori returned to the United States in 1952. [28]

While internees were suffering through the relocation experience and seeing their families disintegrate before their eyes, government officials and those on the outside who had never been to one of the camps, were passing on rumors of "coddling the Japs." Newspapers were full of stories about how good life was

Relocation

inside the camps while the rest of the nation was suffering.

Chapter X

Problems From the Outside

With the arrival of the internees at Heart Mountain, the rumors of the government "coddling the Japs" began almost immediately. Many people on the outside who were ignorant of hardships evacuees faced in the camp, believed, at least some aspect of nearly every rumor that came along. Unlike most newspapers at that time, the *Cody Enterprise* investigated such rumors before printing them. The camp had been open for only three weeks when the *Enterprise* reported that no less than twelve "wild and exciting stories" about the camp were circulating in the area. One of the stories was that 600 residents were planning a revolt at Heart Mountain and were going to attack the MP's and take over the camp. The *Enterprise*, at that time, had investigated seven of the twelve "yarns" and found that none had any foundation. [1]

Naturally, the findings of the *Enterprise* did not satisfy the majority of those who believed the rumors. Wyoming State American Legion Commander, E. J. Goppert of Cody, led a party of Legion members on a trip to Heart Mountain to investigate the "comforts" of the camp. Goppert was accompanied by Powell Legion commander Paul Douglas and Cody attorney, and future Wyoming Governor and U. S. Senator, Milward Simpson. The group said the investigation came about as a result of rumors circulating in Powell and Cody. The guide for the group was Clarence Uno, a World War I veteran and camp internee. The investigators found nothing to support any of the rumors they had heard. [2]

Despite the findings of the American Legion investigating team, some residents of Powell and Cody still believed every rumor that cropped up about the camp. By early December 1942, rumors had it that the government was coddling the "Japs" with washing machines and dishwashers. The only reason that the "Japs" were not able to use the washing machines, according to the rumor-mill, was due to the drain the machines would put on the camp's supply of electricity. [3]

Another prevalent rumor was that "Japs from the center are coming to town and buying knives." [4] Milward Simpson, Park County Civilian Defense Coordinator, led the way in promoting that rumor. Simpson contacted his friend J. S. Bugas, Special Agent in charge of the Detroit Office of the FBI, and told him that local committees were seeking an investigation of Japanese subversives at the Heart Mountain Relocation Center. He said that "Considerable quantities of hand axes, knives, and other instruments [were] being purchased throughout Big Horn Basin by Japanese." [5] Simpson also contacted the War Department to inquire about increasing the number of guards around the camp. [6]

Bugas informed Simpson that the matter had been turned over to the Denver office of the FBI for investigation. He also told the Denver office that

Simpson should be taken seriously because he was a prominent attorney, a member of the University of Wyoming Board of Trustees, and a "super patriot." A special agent from Denver was dispatched to Cody to interview Simpson. During that interview Simpson said that he and a "great many" of Cody's citizens were concerned with the Heart Mountain "situation." The "situation" being the supposed purchase of mass quantities of knives and axes. Nowhere during the conversation did Simpson mention any wrong-doing on the part of local merchants who supposedly sold the weapons to the Japanese. Simpson said that there were 150 soldiers stationed at the camp, but that most of the time there were only five or six on duty. He acknowledged the fact the there had never been any incidents to justify his concern or that of the other concerned citizens of Cody, but he said that they all felt the Japanese were given entirely too much freedom. The town was concerned, according to Simpson, with the protection of the two oil refineries, a power plant, and the area's irrigation project. [7]

The FBI agent contacted the Denver office after his interview with Simpson and an investigation of the situation at Heart Mountain and throughout the Big Horn Basin. The Agent said that at that time he saw no reason for concern. The FBI looked into the purchases made by Japanese who were working in Lovell, Greybull, Manderson and Thermopolis, and found the following: the 250 Japanese working in the Lovell area purchased twenty-two "cheap" butcher or kitchen knives and eleven axes. Nothing was purchased in Thermopolis, and the forty-four internees who worked in the Greybull and Manderson area bought six pocket knives, one ax and a handsaw, according to the sheriff's reports in that county. The FBI agent investigating the matter felt that the purchases were made for the same reasons that any other citizen would buy such items. [8]

The investigating agent not only believed there was no need for concern, he also saw no reason to bother WRA Regional Director Joseph Smart with the matter. The agent did, however, say that he would keep an eye on the situation and keep the Denver office of the FBI and the WRA apprised of any changes. After reading the report filed by the Denver office, FBI Director, J. Edgar Hoover, sent a letter to Edward Ennis, Director of the Alien Enemy Control Unit, and advised Ennis to watch the situation. When no action was taken, Simpson let the issue drop. [9]

After the latest accusations and hysteria, John Nelson, a senior administrative official at the camp, said the attitude in Cody toward the center was getting worse. Jack Richard, editor of the *Cody Enterprise*, traveled to Heart Mountain many times and had cooperated completely with camp officials. After Simpson's allegations, Richard no longer came around. Nelson observed that it was strange how the internees were great people when the locals needed their crops harvested, but once that was finished, they were, "dirty yellow rats." [10] It had been only a short time since the merchants of Powell and Cody contemplated running buses from their respective towns to the camp and back in order to get the

One of nine guard towers on the perimeter of the Heart Mountain Relocation Center (JR-BSC).

internees to spend their money in area businesses. That idea was no longer being discussed. Nelson correctly predicted that when the sugar beets needed thinning the next summer, internees would once again be seen as "nice people" by the locals. [11]

Although rumors regarding Heart Mountain circulated throughout the Big Horn Basin and the rest of Wyoming, they were most prominent in and around the communities of Powell and Cody. And though individuals in both towns believed at least some of what they heard about the camp, this was more the case in Cody, than in Powell. With the exception of local politicians, many Powell residents saw the Heart Mountain internees as little more than a curiosity. This was due, in large part, to the efforts of *Powell Tribune* editor Ray Baird and Heart Mountain internee, Mary Oyama Mittwer. Baird believed that the internees at Heart Mountain belonged in the camp. However, he also understood that a congenial relationship between the residents of the camp and the town of Powell would be of economic benefit to the community. Mittwer, on the other hand, felt that good relations with any community outside the camp would be of benefit to the internees. A trip made by camp residents to a friendly town would be a vacation from the monotony of camp life.

During the first week of November 1942, Mittwer began writing a column for the *Powell Tribune* titled, "Heart Mountain Breezes" under her maiden name, Mary Oyama. Oyama began her first column with, "Howdy: Greetings fellow Americans of Wyoming!" [12] Throughout her first column, Oyama described the beauty of the Heart Mountain area with its picturesque sunrises and sunsets. She cast her fellow internees as "greenhorns" and explained how the children were unaccustomed to seeing sheep, cattle and snow. After sucking the reader in with compliments about the natural beauty of northwest Wyoming, Oyama gracefully pointed out that the residents of Heart Mountain were not "Japs," but "Americans with Japanese faces." [13] From her first column, throughout her stay at Heart Mountain, Oyama, with her down-home and folksy writing style, endeared herself to the *Tribune*'s readers. Powell politicians had their own agenda as far as the camp was concerned, and some residents bought into the rumors that circulated about the center. But through Oyama's writing, which historian Douglas Nelson has described as "a brilliant piece of propaganda work . . . ," [14] most residents of Powell never gave the camp a second thought. However, the exceptions to the rule did surface.

In mid December, Mrs. Howard Galvin, leader of the "War Mothers of Powell," contacted Milward Simpson of Cody to find out what was going on at Heart Mountain. Galvin had heard numerous rumors of superior treatment of internees at the camp. She asked Simpson if he could shed some light on the matter. Her biggest concern was that those on the outside were having their food rationed while internees were receiving whatever they wanted. Simpson assured Galvin that the same rationing controls were in effect on both sides of the fence. [15] Simpson's attitude had mellowed somewhat in the three weeks since he feared that knife and ax wielding internees would swoop down on Cody's oil refineries and destroy them. And to Simpson's credit, he was not so quick to buy into such rumors in the future. At times he even went to some length to dispel such stories. In spite of a temporary change in attitude, Simpson worked hard to insure that the Japanese were removed from Wyoming following the conclusion of the war. In a letter to Senator O'Mahoney in April of 1944 Simpson described the residents of Heart Mountain as "a sullen and nasty lot; . . ." [16]

Family making one of many daily trips to the mess hall, latrine or laundry. Drawing by Estelle Ishigo (BSC).

As if the rumors about the center were not causing enough problems for the internees and the camp's administrators, the editor of the Powell newspaper was trying to play down hardships being faced by Heart Mountain residents. While he never believed the rumors which circulated about Heart Mountain, R. T. Baird was always one to promote the rough life of the "rugged individuals" who settled in the Powell area. In an editorial, he said that if there were hardships and discomforts for internees, they should keep in mind that in "Wyoming's Garden Spot" they were safe from the war. He added that the hardships evacuees thought they were enduring were nothing compared to those suffered by early settlers in the Powell Valley. A Mrs. "J" of Powell quickly bought into Baird's propaganda and pointed out that she had to raise her two sons without the use of electric appliances, a definite hardship. In her weekly column about camp life for the *Powell Tribune*, Mary Oyama tactfully pointed out to Baird and Mrs. "J," that pioneers came to the Powell Valley of their own free will. The people who faced hardship in the early years had a choice, and that, Oyama said, was the distinct difference between the pioneers and the internees. [17]

While the rumors of coddling and pampering the "Japs" were on the increase in the areas surrounding Heart Mountain and other camps, they were running rampant in the nation's capital. Many senators, mostly Republicans, were calling for an investigation of the WRA and of the relocation centers themselves. John Nelson said he would welcome an investigation and visitation of the camps. He said that congressmen would see old men and old women along with infant children being forced to walk a block or more in twenty-five to thirty below zero temperatures to get to the mess hall for meals. Those trips would be made many times each day in order to get to the community latrine, laundry, and shower. Nelson felt that the congressmen should also eat the substandard, and at times, poorly prepared food that was all the evacuees had. Nelson wanted the congressmen to explain to the Japanese American citizens why they were removed from their homes and placed in concentration camps when they had not been charged with any crime or given a trial. Lastly, Nelson believed the congressmen should explain why Japanese aliens were put in concentration camps while German and Italian aliens were not. [18]

When the Wyoming State Legislature met in January of 1943, Senator George Burke of Powell introduced a bill which would prevent the residents of Heart Mountain from voting in Wyoming elections. The reason given for the introduction of the bill was that there were thousands of internees in the camp who were American citizens that would soon qualify to vote if they were not prevented from doing so. Burke's bill, which stated,

> that each citizen of the United States who has been or is hereafter brought, or caused to be brought, into the State of Wyoming by the War Relocation Authority, or any similar agency, and who is now or hereafter interned in a relocation center or concentration camp or any other similar governmental facility established in Wyoming under any national emergency which has been or is hereafter proclaimed by the president of the United States, shall be prohibited from voting in any election in the State of Wyoming . . . . [19]

was approved on February 5, 1943 and was signed into law by Governor Lester Hunt. Another bill was also pending which would prevent aliens "ineligible to citizenship" from purchasing land in Wyoming. The law, however, contained the stipulation that Chinese people could purchase land in Wyoming since they were our allies in the war against Japan. [20]

On February 6, 1943, Special Agent Gordon Nicholson of the FBI office in Denver, wrote to J. Edgar Hoover concerning an interview which had taken place between an agent in Cody and an assistant steward at Heart Mountain. The interview between the agent and Earl Alfred Best, the steward, was the first step in a major smear campaign against the camp. Best informed the agent that Japanese cooks in the center would go to the warehouse daily and order food even though they had great quantities hidden in the attics and other secret compartments within each mess hall. Best claimed he had carried out an inventory of a number of the mess halls and on one occasion was attacked by one of the Japanese cooks for doing so. Best's inventories showed that the mess halls had an average of $2,000 worth of food hidden in attics and different compartments. He told the agent that there was no reason for such large inventories. [21]

Best also claimed that there was a great waste of food inside the camp. Whole hams had been stored in mess hall attics and allowed to spoil. While the FBI took a great deal of interest in Best's story, it did not feel that there was any proof of wrong-doing or mismanagement, and no action was taken against the WRA or camp officials. [22]

Best had recently been terminated from his position of assistant steward at Heart Mountain and after no action was taken against the camp by the FBI, he made a similar report to the *Denver Post*. In April, the *Post* contacted camp director Guy Robertson, and asked for permission to send an investigative reporter up to tour the facilities. Robertson contacted Governor Lester Hunt and informed him that the *Post* reporter, Jack Carberry, had "arrived on schedule, made a complete and exhaustive survey of our project, mostly from the Irma Hotel [in Cody]." [23] Robertson told Hunt that he expected a "grand smear." [24]

Robertson was not disappointed in his expectations of a "grand smear." Jack Carberry wrote a series of articles concerning the waste and hoarding of food at Heart Mountain. Carberry, a sports writer, came to the conclusion that there was enough food at Heart Mountain to last for three years, six months and fourteen days. Carberry never explained how he arrived at those figures. He also said that there was $12,000 worth of baby food and only five babies in the hospital. That, according to Carberry, was definite proof of hoarding. Bill Hosokawa said that Carberry was the *Post*'s hatchet man and had been sent to Heart Mountain to "gut the camp." [25]

Robertson answered all of the *Post*'s accusations immediately. He told newspaper reporters that the camp had $252,133 worth of food on hand. The director explained that it was costing, on average, $120,000 per month to feed the almost 11,000 residents of the center, and that the orders for food from the Quarter Master Corps had to be placed 50 days in advance. It was therefore necessary to have a two-month supply of food on hand. Robertson pointed out that the supply of baby food, which Carberry found, was for the 450 children in the camp who were under the age of two. The five newborn babies in the hospital did not eat baby food. While the WRA had set an allowance of 45 cents as the amount which could be spent on meals for one person each day, Heart Mountain was spending only 36.8 cents per day. Even that figure is somewhat misleading because the army was paying extremely high prices for the food it was sending to Heart Mountain. John Nelson said that the army paid 43 cents per dozen for eggs and then shipped them to the camp. A dozen eggs purchased in Powell cost less than 30 cents. [26]

Despite Guy Robertson's efforts, the damage had been done. The *Denver Post* continued to write false articles about Heart Mountain for several weeks. Those articles were grabbed up by Republican congressmen and senators as evidence of mismanagement and coddling. One of the most outspoken of those individuals was Wyoming's, recently elected, junior United States Senator, Edward V. Robertson of Cody. Senator Robertson attacked the camp and its inhabitants viciously in the newspapers even though he had never set foot inside the center himself. [27]

Senator Robertson told the *Denver Post* that the Japanese were being fed better than any American on the outside. He said there was no rationing in the camp, and there was a great deal of waste. He even went so far as to say that many of the residents had their own cars and were given unlimited freedom to drive to Powell or Cody. According John Nelson, Robertson got most of his information from his friends in Cody. On May 6, 1943 Robertson made a speech on the floor of the U. S. Senate in which he stated that the situation at Heart Mountain could quite easily get out of control. He added that the Japanese should be treated as prisoners of war whether they were American citizens or not, and that people were not going to stand by and do nothing while the Japanese were "petted and pampered." [28]

Senator Robertson was in Cody early in June and had lunch with James Porter, one of the camp's administrators. Porter invited Robertson to come out and visit the camp so that he could see for himself how it was being run. The senator informed Porter that he was too busy. Governors Smith and Hunt, and Senator Joseph C. O'Mahoney were all able to make the 800 mile round trip from Cheyenne to Heart Mountain for fact finding tours. But Senator Robertson was too busy to make a twenty-six mile round trip from Cody to the camp. Another formal invitation was sent to Robertson in the form of a 191 word telegram which, according to Western Union, the senator signed for himself. He never did reply to the telegram. [29]

One month later, Robertson was in Cody again while the Senate was in recess. He was apparently still "too busy" to visit Heart Mountain, but he did have time to discuss the camp with members of the Cody Chamber of Commerce. The senator told the group that the WRA realized how inefficient it was and would soon separate the loyal Japanese from the disloyal. Robertson said the disloyal would be sent to a segregation center (Tule Lake) while the loyal Japanese "would be rehabilitated" and the camp abandoned. It was his belief that the center would be turned into a prisoner-of-war camp. [30]

Robertson turned down another invitation to visit the camp and continued to denigrate the Japanese and Japanese Americans at Heart Mountain. The senator told the *Denver Post* that he would like to see all American citizens of Japanese ancestry deported. He added that there might be some problems in getting around the Constitution when trying to deport the undesirables. Why would Robertson, a United States Senator sworn to uphold the Constitution, be looking for a way to subvert it? To the Japanese Americans at Heart Mountain who had been the focus of Robertson's lies and false accusations, the answer was simple. They were American citizens by birth. Robertson was a foreigner, born in Wales, who came to the United States seeking opportunity. Even after settling in Park County, Wyoming, Robertson did not apply for U. S. citizenship for fourteen years. Japanese Americans felt it was bad enough that their constitutional rights were being ignored by other Americans. But when a foreigner was using outright lies to try to side-step the Constitution in order to have them deported they asked, "Can there be any honor in the soul of a man who would condemn totally any minority group without first weighing carefully all of the evidence?"[31]

Wyoming's Congressman, Frank Barrett, not to be outdone by Robertson, declared on the floor of the House of Representatives that Wyoming officials agreed to the internment of Japanese in the state only if they were sent back to California following the war. He told Congress that the people of Wyoming did not like the "fact" that the Japanese were being fed better than they were. Several members of the California delegation rose immediately and said that they did not want the Japanese removed from Wyoming and especially not back to California.[32]

The articles in the *Denver Post* and frequent statements made by men like E. V. Robertson and Frank Barrett, led to congressmen sitting on the "Dies Committee for un-American Activities" to make even more bizarre and outrageous statements. The Dies Committee, which according to John Kitasako, who took over Mary Oyama's column in the *Powell Tribune* when she relocated, was in the business of "lie manufacturing." The Committee said that evacuees were receiving prime beef and five gallons of whiskey each. They also said that thousands of the Japanese being relocated were trained in sabotage in Tokyo by a group known as the "Black Dragon Society."[33]

Earl Best was the darling of the *Denver Post* and was even named to that newspaper's hall of fame. His accusations led to the Carberry investigation, and he eventually became a key witness for the Dies Committee when it was investigating the relocation centers. After Best's sensational rise in popularity among those trying to bring down the WRA, he was arrested in Los Angeles in September 1943 on charges of forgery. He was also found to be an illegal alien. It was the second time he had entered the United States illegally. Following his trial on forgery charges, Best was deported to Canada.[34]

The lies and accusations made concerning Heart Mountain on the national level, combined with false statements put forward by Earl Best, Jack Carberry, and

Senator E. V. Robertson, contributed to a hysteria within the state of Wyoming and some calls for the deportation of all people of Japanese ancestry. The first lady, Eleanor Roosevelt, said there was no coddling of the Japanese in any of the camps, and added that, "I would not choose their situation as a way to live." [35] Although those were not words many people wanted to hear, some individuals and newspapers did support the residents of Heart Mountain.

Wyoming newspapers picked up the stories printed in the *Denver Post* and the accusations made by Earl Best and Senator E. V. Robertson. Running those stories, as many papers in the state did, caused an uproar among newspaper editors and less informed readers throughout Wyoming. L. L. Newton, editor of the *Wyoming State Journal* in Lander, was the only newspaper editor in the state to say from the very beginning, that the whole relocation process was unconstitutional and a violation of the internees' rights. Newton had little regard for comments by Senator Robertson, Earl Best, the Dies Committee or the *Denver Post*. The *Casper Tribune-Herald* argued that "No Caucasian would want to trade places [with an internee] . . . ." The editor of the *Lovell Chronicle* suggested that the Dies Committee investigate the *Denver Post* instead of the Heart Mountain Relocation Center. Scott Taggart of Cody said that both the *Post* and Robertson were wrong. Powell attorney Lowell Stephens found it interesting that Robertson could address a crowd in Philadelphia concerning the problems at Heart Mountain, yet was too busy to drive out to the camp when he visited Cody. [36] But those who found fault with Robertson and the *Post* were in the minority.

William Stone, a Casper attorney, asked Governor Hunt to lead the state in a fight against the food storage problem at the "Cody Jap camp." [37] Hunt informed Stone that the *Post* was only writing a political story and that he was not interested in "political skullduggery." [38] After giving Stone many of the same figures that Guy Robertson used to refute the Carberry article, Hunt said that he was looking more at the political motivation behind the story and not whether "the Japs have one or two months' supply of food on hand." [39] Harold Waechter of the International Association of Machinists in Cheyenne told the governor that their membership was very upset with the scandalous articles which appeared in the local papers concerning the Japanese situation. He stated that while his group was not in possession of the actual facts concerning the camp, they still believed that the center should be put under military control. Military control, according to Waechter, "would be more practical for these undesirables, . . ." [40]

Governor Hunt also heard from the Rock Springs post of the VFW. The post's members, who were obviously influenced by Senator Robertson's comments concerning the deportation of all people of Japanese ancestry, adopted a resolution which they presented to Hunt. The resolution stated that it was a known fact that many American-born Japanese were fighting in the Japanese army. That many Americans had died while "fighting these fanatical Emperor worshiping maniacs, . . ." [41] It was therefore decided that, all Japanese be placed in concentration camps and treated as prisoners of war; [and] That legislation be initiated immediately to remove all Japanese from the United States within six months following the close of the war; . . . [42]

The VFW was adopting the same resolution which had been written by another post in Ogden, Utah. That group stated that its new members who had fought on Guadalcanal informed them of the "treachery of the Japs." [43] They told Hunt that it was up to him to help remedy the injustices which the Japanese had caused. [44]

The lies and accusations which were aimed at Heart Mountain and its residents by Carberry, Best, and E. V. Robertson, had an adverse impact on the camp up to the time it closed. However, that adverse impact, in the form of negative attitudes toward the camp and its residents, did not manifest itself in the majority of the general population in surrounding communities. In Powell, this was due in large part to the work of Mary Oyama. In time, the general public seemed to adopt an attitude of indifference toward Heart Mountain. The negative attitudes, and at times, outright hatred, took root with a handful of local politicians and a few of their followers. Despite the fact that many internees volunteered for and were drafted into the army where they fought and died for a country that kept their parents behind barbed wire, the negative comments from the outside continued.

Chapter XI

Nisei in the Army

During the summer of 1940, Congress adopted the nations's first peacetime conscription law. This was one of the first federal laws enacted which contained a "non-discrimination clause." The clause, however, had no value once the individual entered the service as Blacks, and later, Japanese Americans, were quickly moved into segregated units. All Americans between the ages of twenty-one and thirty-six were required to register for Selective Service (the draft). Some Japanese Americans enlisted or were drafted prior to the bombing of Pearl Harbor. Shortly after that attack, some military commands discharged Japanese Americans already serving, while draft boards reclassified others of Japanese ancestry. [1] Initially Japanese Americans were designated "4-F (those physically, mentally or morally unfit), and later as 4-C (not acceptable for military service because of nationality or ancestry)." [2]

Despite the draft designation of 4-C and the fact that Japanese Americans were incarcerated behind barbed wire, they were still required to register with Selective Service after they reached the relocation centers. The sixth registration for those eighteen and nineteen years of age was completed at Heart Mountain on December 31, 1942. It was a type of catch-up operation in which the younger men, and those who could not register while in assembly centers, were registered. Those who turned eighteen after January 1 were to register on their birthday, and anyone who did not register had his name turned over to the district attorney. In a short time, the draft registration age was lowered to seventeen, and Heart Mountain internees in that age group were also registered. [3]

By the end of 1942, rumors were circulating that a segregated force of Japanese American soldiers was to be organized. Many Nisei welcomed the opportunity to serve in the armed forces, although by the middle of February 1943, Secretary of War, Henry Stimson, was trying to answer the question, "why a segregated unit?" Americans of Japanese ancestry also wanted to know if they would be allowed to fight in the same areas as Caucasian troops. Stimson said that a segregated unit was being formed, "only because the War Department desires to aid the loyal American-Japanese . . . ." [4] He added that many millions of Americans were not familiar with Japanese Americans and that if they were spread throughout the armed forces with Caucasians they would go unnoticed. According to Stimson, a segregated unit that fought well would receive valuable recognition which could be used to illustrate Japanese American loyalty. Another example of loyalty and patriotism would be seen in the fact that this was to be an all-volunteer unit. [5] Stimson said that the, "success of the program and the voluntary feature of induction will be a great step forward in the rehabilitation

. . . [of] American-Japanese." [6] An interesting point here was that throughout the war there was reference by the government and civilians to the, "rehabilitation" of Japanese Americans. What was missing was an explanation as to why they required rehabilitation.

Early 1943 was also the time of the loyalty questionnaire (discussed in a previous chapter). The focus, again, was on questions twenty-seven and twenty-eight. While the phrasing of the questions was not changed, Lt. Ray McDaniel, sent to Heart Mountain to recruit volunteers for the all Nisei army unit, said that a "Yes" answer to question twenty-seven (will you serve in combat?) did not mean that one was volunteering for the army. Some of those who answered questions twenty-seven and twenty-eight added conditions. To question twenty-seven, some answered, "Yes, if my constitutional rights are restored and I can return to my home." That was not an acceptable answer. A straight "Yes" or "No" was required. To be seen by the government as loyal and to be able to volunteer for the segregated army unit, one had to give an unconditional "Yes" to both questions (a qualified "Yes" was later allowed). [7]

In 1943, when Henry Stimson asked Japanese Americans to join the all Nisei unit, the army was calling for 1,500 volunteers from Hawaii. After only two weeks, 7,425 had signed up in the hope of being accepted. The response was not as positive among Japanese Americans on the mainland. The nearly 150,000 people of Japanese ancestry in Hawaii, except for approximately 1,500 whom the FBI apprehended following the attack on Pearl Harbor, had not been rounded up and forced to leave their homes. People of Japanese ancestry in Hawaii were seen by the military commander there as an asset to both the economy and the war effort. Because of General DeWitt's fear of a Japanese invasion of the West Coast, the Japanese Americans on the mainland had been forcibly removed from their homes and placed behind barbed wire, and they were very suspicious of any government programs. [8]

Heart Mountain Project Director, Guy Robertson, urged the camp's male residents to volunteer for the army, but very few did. Robertson sent a letter to all block chairmen and block managers telling them that it was not his duty to induce men to volunteer. He placed that responsibility on the parents of the young men in camp. Robertson pointed out that Heart Mountain had been considered a model for all other relocation centers, but with the small turnout of volunteers it could no longer "claim favorable recognition . . . ." [9] The director tried to push the parents of volunteer age men by telling them that their children might be marked for life if they did not, "live up to their responsibility in a democratic government . . . ." [10] The threats of a stigma that might be borne by those who did not carry their weight in a democratic country had little influence on people forced to live behind barbed wire.

Robertson told the people of Heart Mountain that they had one of the lowest turn-outs of volunteers of all ten camps. He said that the residents could not expect to be treated favorably by the government if they were not going to support government sponsored programs. However, it was not too late at that time to remedy the situation. He urged the people to do everything in their power so that the report on volunteers would not look as unfavorable as it did at that time. [11]

The following day, in his report to WRA Director, Dillon Myer, Robertson said that the registration program for volunteers was almost complete. As of March 6, 1943, only thirty-eight men had volunteered. Robertson believed that some sort of resistance group or individual was responsible for the poor showing, but a number of small investigations failed to reveal any evidence to support that view. After meeting with several internee groups he received no "enthusiastic support" for the volunteer program. [12] Unable to find any specific group or individual responsible for encouraging young men not to volunteer for military service, Robertson called for a camp-wide investigation. Although the investigation revealed very little to the administration, many volunteer-aged Nisei were influenced by a group known as the Heart Mountain Congress of American Citizens (this group will be discussed in detail in the following chapter).

After going over all available information and interviewing a number of evacuees, the investigator made several findings which were reported to the project director. A great majority of Heart Mountain residents were very bitter over the fact that they had been forcibly removed from their homes simply on the basis of race. They did not appreciate the baseless attacks made on them in newspapers and by congressmen and government officials. Internees also expressed displeasure with the people of Cody. A number of businesses had signs that said "No Japs," and any reference to the residents of Heart Mountain by many Cody merchants or officials either began or ended with, "The Goddamned Japs." [13]

The report also found that the internees were very suspicious of army programs in general. After all, it was the army that had removed them from their homes. Another issue which bothered evacuees was the phrasing of questions twenty-seven and twenty-eight on the loyalty questionnaire. And most importantly, they wanted clarification of their citizenship rights. Internees failed to see why they were not allowed the rights and freedoms of their American citizenship and yet could still be castigated for not volunteering to join the army. The problem was best described by Toyoo Nitake and Frank Hayami. Both men said that the government was quick to point out that as citizens of the United States either they, or their brothers, should fight to defend the nation. They were expected to put their lives on the line so that their parents would have the right to live behind barbed wire. [14]

One of the big problems which made internees more resentful and suspicious of the army was the way in which the volunteer registration was carried out. The army sent a mere lieutenant to explain and take care of the process. The evacuees saw that as an insult. They did not understand why they should rush to sign up for the army if a lieutenant was the highest ranking officer that Washington could send, even though the residents personally liked Lieutenant McDaniel. McDaniel himself admitted that those who sent him on the job did not give him the proper background or preparation for what he was supposed to accomplish. [15]

In the end, the report placed much of the blame for lack of volunteers on the camp's administration. It stated that the internees felt they were being treated in an inferior manner. To them this was made clear by administrators in certain statements such as "It's about time we get hard boiled." "A Jap's a Jap. This proves it." "They don't appreciate what we do for them." "Might as well drop this sentimental attitude and be realistic." [16]

The army left the situation as it was for nearly a year. The volunteers from Hawaii made up the 100th Infantry Battalion. By October 1943, the 100th infantry began making a name for itself. In its first action along the Volturno front in the mountains north of Benevento, Italy the 100th was receiving high praise. After suffering heavy casualties, the 100th received replacements from the 442nd, many of whom came from the relocation centers. The 100th Infantry and the 522nd Field Artillery would become elements of the 442nd Regimental Combat Team, the "Go for Broke" boys. The segregated Japanese American unit would become the most highly decorated unit for its size and time in service in U. S. Army history. [17]

In January 1944, the federal government authorized the Selective Service to reclassify the draft status of all Nisei previously designated as 4-C. The new classification given Japanese Americans was 1-A. It meant that all Japanese Americans were eligible for the draft and subject to Selective Service laws. This action was taken when volunteer replacements for the 442nd could not be found in sufficient numbers (the unit suffered 300% casualties during the war). Gene Kumagai was the first resident of Heart Mountain to receive his induction notice. It was not long before more than thirty Heart Mountain men were sent to Fort Warren in Cheyenne for their preinduction physicals. Of that group, only Sam Fujishin passed his physical. Since only one man had been accepted, it was believed that the Nisei were not going to be drafted. However, Guy Robertson and army officials eventually had inductees sent to Denver for physicals. In Denver, nearly everyone was accepted. According to Fujishin, some of those conducting the physicals at Fort Warren were Navy doctors who had been at Pearl Harbor on December 7. [18]

Sam Fujishin was the first draftee to leave Heart Mountain for service in the army. Before he departed, however, he attended a meeting of the Fair Play Committee with his father (this group believed that they should not serve in the army until their civil rights were restored; the group will be looked at in detail in the next chapter). Fujishin said he decided before attending the meeting that he would report to the army. But before leaving, his father wanted him to be aware of all positions concerning the draft prevalent in camp at that time. Fujishin left Heart Mountain without much fanfare. Later, as the number of men being drafted increased, there were community farewell gatherings and patriotic speeches made for the inductees. [19]

Despite the growing number of draftees entering into the army from Heart

The Heart Mountain USO (ERC).

Mountain, there was still resentment over questions twenty-seven and twenty-eight on the loyalty questionnaire in spite of finally being allowed to qualify one's answers. Jack Oda wondered why question twenty-eight did not ask, "Will you swear allegiance to the United States?" Oda and others were also curious as to why German-Americans or Italian-Americans did not have to foreswear allegiance to Adolf Hitler or Mussolini. [20]

Resentment over a number of issues sometimes made for ticklish situations. When one of Oda's friends was leaving camp for service in the army approximately fifteen of the young draftee's friends tried to walk him to the bus to say good-bye. The men walked through the front gate with their friend, but none of them had passes. A jeep load of armed MP's immediately raced out the gate and ordered the men back to camp at rifle point. Following that incident Oda and others complained to the administration. From that time on, passes were issued so that friends and family members could see the men off. The young man who was going to catch the bus was later in the 442nd Honor Guard when the unit was reviewed by President Truman and given another Presidential Unit Citation. [21]

Frank Hayami left Heart Mountain and was working in New York when the government reclassified Japanese Americans from 4-C to 1-A. Hayami was drafted into the army in New York. His younger brother, Stan, a recent graduate of Heart Mountain High School, was drafted out of the camp at Heart Mountain. Both men later were wounded in the same battle in Italy. Frank Hayami recovered from his wounds, but his brother died. Stan Hayami was one of twenty-two men from Heart Mountain who gave their lives for their country. Mrs. Hayami received the news that her son had been killed in action, not in her own home in California, but behind the barbed wire confines of a concentration camp in Northwest Wyoming. [22]

Kaoru Inouye, Heart Mountain High School's hard working chemistry teacher, was drafted into the army in August 1944. Unlike most Japanese Americans who were a part of the 442nd and fought in the European Theater, Inouye was one of about 6,000 American soldiers of Japanese ancestry who served in the Pacific Theater. Men who fell into that group were usually sent to language school and then attached to army intelligence where they interrogated prisoners or translated captured Japanese documents. According to General Willoughby, of MacArthur's staff, there was never any period in American History when the army knew more about its enemy prior to engaging in battle than in the Pacific during World War II. Much of that knowledge about the enemy was a direct result of work carried out by Japanese American soldiers. Following the war, many of those men were part of American occupation forces in Japan. Inouye, who was discharged from the army following the conclusion of hostilities, worked for the government as a civilian chemical investigator throughout occupied Japan. [23]

While the heroics and legend of the 442nd grew daily, some Japanese Americans wanted to join the navy. In a speech given at Heart Mountain, Ernest Goppert, Wyoming State Commander of the American Legion, mistakenly said that the Nisei could join any branch of the service they wished. However, Secretary of the Navy, Frank Knox, was not allowing Japanese Americans to join the navy. He said that it would cause a great number of racial problems and that the mission of the navy was far more important than the rights of Japanese Americans. [24] It should be remembered that Knox wrongly credited the successful Japanese attack on Pearl Harbor to Japanese American saboteurs and fifth columnists.

In Hood River, Oregon, the names of sixteen Japanese Americans were removed from that town's American Legion Memorial Honor Roll. After criticism from newspapers in Washington and Oregon and especially from the Texas 36th Division, fifteen of the names were restored to the monument (the record does not indicate why only fifteen of the names were restored). The "Lost Battalion"

The Yamano family. The son, on leave from the army, returned to Heart Mountain for a visit (JR-BSC).

was part of the Texas 36th Division. The battalion had been surrounded and cut off by German troops in Southern France near the town of Bruyeres. They held out for more than a week while elements of the 442nd suffered heavy casualties in effecting their rescue. In fact, the 442nd suffered three times more dead and wounded than the number of soldiers rescued. Those serving in the Texas 36th had no sympathy with the actions taken by the Hood River, American Legion. [25]

The rescued soldiers of the Lost Battalion were not the only ones who appreciated the efforts of Japanese American soldiers. Following the conclusion of the war, the remains of American soldiers were sent to the United States for reburial. However, the townspeople of Bruyeres wanted to keep the grave of one Japanese American soldier to remind them, and future generations, of the brave men who fought and died to liberate their town. A petition was sent to the parents of Tomosu Hirahara, the first Nisei killed in the battle for Bruyeres. After considering the request, Hirahara family consented. Staff Sergeant Hirahara's grave is still carefully tended today. [26]

In spite of the bravery exhibited and the high casualties suffered by the 442nd during its relief of the Lost Battalion, it was late November, 1944, nearly one month after the rescue, before the public was informed that the 36th was relieved by Japanese American troops. Even though members of the 442nd were interviewed by reporters, they were described as the relief unit or another unit. One Japanese American soldier was listed by the interviewing reporter as, a private who wasn't a Jerry. This censorship could only have been approved at the highest levels of command. At the time of the relief, it was still not politically expedient to promote the exploits of soldiers whose friends and relatives were locked behind barbed wire in the United States. Newsreels showing that it was the 442nd which effected the relief of the Lost Battalion, were finally released to the public just days before President Roosevelt announced that Japanese Americans could leave the camps and return to the West Coast. [27] That announcement came one day prior to the Supreme Court's ruling that it was illegal to hold Japanese Americans in camps against their will.

The survivors of the Dachau death camp remembered seeing Japanese faces in American uniforms. Members of the Japanese American 522nd Field Artillery Unit were among the first U. S. troops to liberate the Nazi death camp. Clarence Matsumura was among the first to walk through the gates of Dachau. Matsumura's life, from December 7, 1941, until the end of the war, was one of strange irony. [28]

Clarence Matsumura was born in a small town in Wyoming. His family moved to Southern California when he was young, but with the outbreak of World War II, Matsumura and his family returned to Wyoming. But this was a forced move to Heart Mountain Relocation Center. Matsumura was at Heart Mountain for a year before deciding to enlist in the army. Upon completion of basic training, he was assigned to 522nd Field Artillery Unit, serving in Italy and France. [29]

The Army

Following the liberation of Bruyeres and the relief of the "Lost Battalion," the push toward Germany continued. The 522nd's forward observers often served as scouts for the advancing Seventh, and sometimes Third, armies. During the late spring of 1945, the German Army decided to use slave labor to build fortifications to slow the advancing Americans. Solly Ganor, a Lithuanian Jew, was one of those taken from Lager Ten, one of Dachau's satellite camps, and force marched to the main camp. During the last week of April, 1945, Ganor, his father, and thousands of other Jews and Russian prisoners of war, were marched out of Dachau toward the advancing Americans. After marching for several days, with stragglers being shot by soldiers or killed by guard dogs, the slave laborers were bedded down in a field. [30]

After seeing two of his traveling companions killed during the march, Solly Ganor lay down in the field, covered himself in his wet blanket and went to sleep. He awoke several times during the night to the sound of gun shots, but by morning, May 2, 1945, it was strangely quiet. Ganor crawled out from under his snow covered blanket, and to his astonishment, saw oriental soldiers walking toward him. One of the soldiers knelt down, put his hand on Ganor's shoulder and said, "You are free, boy. You're free now, . . ." The confused Ganor could only mumble, "Who? . . ." The soldier smiled, a smile Ganor would never forget, and said, "Americans. Americans, Nisei. Japanese Americans. My name is Clarence." [31] After taking Ganor and other prisoners back the American's main camp, Clarence Matsumura and others proceeded on to Dachau.

Matsumura said it was strange walking through the gates of Dachau. The barbed wire and hastily built wooden barracks looked somewhat familiar. While he was helping to care for Jews who had been sent to Dachau because of their race, his parents still languished at Heart Mountain. [32] There are only physical similarities between Dachau and Heart Mountain. Dachau was a Nazi death camp while Heart Mountain was a relocation center. There is not the slightest comparison in how the residents of each camp were treated, but in both cases the people of the camps had their rights abrogated and were locked up solely on the basis of race.

More than 900 men and women from Heart Mountain served in the armed forces during World War II. Some were drafted or volunteered after they had relocated, but 654 went directly from camp into the service. [33] The men and women from Heart Mountain contributed greatly to ending the war in the Pacific and to the almost mythic legend of the 442nd. They were not only fighting America's enemies, they were fighting for acceptance as American citizens.

Once, on a visit to Heart Mountain, a young Catholic priest, Father John Meyer, recalled seeing Nisei soldiers returning to camp to visit family members. He said,

> these young bright men, clad proudly in the uniform of our country, would pass through the barbed wire gate to visit their loved ones. Said

gate was being guarded by other young men, clad in the same type and color uniform of our country. (They say that 'War makes for strange bedfellows.' How true that was at Heart Mountain in the 40's in a numbing hurting way for so many Americans, whose only fault was that they were of Japanese decent.) [34]

Many residents of Heart Mountain, through hard work and deeds of bravery on the battle field, fought for acceptance in American society despite the fact that the great majority were already American citizens. However, a few men decided to stand up to the government which had put them behind barbed wire. They made their stand by fighting the draft. These men said they would gladly fight for America when their rights as American citizens were recognized, but not until then.

Chapter XII

The Draft Resisters

During the early months of 1944, when the change in draft status from 4-C to 1-A made Americans of Japanese ancestry eligible for induction into the army, an organization was formed at Heart Mountain known as the "Fair Play Committee" (FPC). With the loss of their civil rights, the FPC and its members felt no obligation to serve in the armed forces of the United States. The members of the group wanted the government to clarify their status as citizens, and a return of internees' civil rights. In other words, if the government considered Japanese Americans citizens as far as the draft laws were concerned, then FPC members felt they should be recognized as citizens in every sense of the word. If their rights were fully restored, FPC members said they would gladly comply with the requirements of the Selective Service Act. On the other hand, if those rights were not restored and Japanese Americans continued to be treated as citizens only when it was to the government's advantage, they felt no obligation to comply with the laws of Selective Service. [1]

The FPC had its roots in another, short lived, organization in camp known as "The Heart Mountain Congress of American Citizens." The Congress, led by Frank Inouye, a senior at UCLA at the time of evacuation, came about as a result of the loyalty questionnaire and the army's search for volunteers at Heart Mountain. At a community meeting, in February of 1943, when Lieutenant McDaniels was calling for volunteers to join the army, Inouye asked McDaniels how he could expect people who had been illegally removed from their homes and locked away, to volunteer for service in the army. "Inouye called for the formation of an elected central body . . . " to discuss the internees' current situation and the government's request for volunteers. [2]

On February 11, at the group's first meeting, Inouye was elected chairman and Paul Nakadate, secretary. Other notable individuals in attendance were Kiyoshi Okamoto and Frank S. Emi. The stand taken by the Congress resulted in only thirty-eight individuals volunteering for service in the army. Of that number, "nineteen were eventually inducted." The Congress did achieve a moral victory when the army changed its policy and allowed conditioned responses to questions twenty-seven and twenty-eight of the loyalty questionnaire. Inouye felt that the most significant result of the Congress's short existence was the work carried on by the Fair Play Committee one year later. [3]

Kiyoshi Okamoto, leader of the FPC, began organizing and holding meetings at Heart Mountain shortly after the government changed the draft designation for Japanese Americans. When that change went into effect, there were three different points of view in the camp, according to FBI agent Harry McMillen.

The first point of view was taken by a small minority who welcomed the draft as a step toward restoration of full civil rights despite the "discriminatory features" (McMillen's words). The minority viewpoint from the other end of the spectrum was that taken by Okamoto and the FPC. They felt that the Nisei had no obligation to the government until all injustices which occurred under the relocation process were erased. The majority believed, according to McMillen, that the drafting of evacuees from a camp where they had been placed without their consent was most unfair. Nevertheless, they also felt that they would have to go along with the draft or they would be punished, and the anti-Japanese sentiment on the outside would increase. Okamoto and the FPC tried to convince that group that it was time for the Nisei to stand up for their rights. [4]

By mid February, 1944, the FPC was holding regular meetings. Camp Director Guy Robertson tried to find individuals who attended FPC meetings to come forward and testify as to what Okamoto was preaching. Robertson was attempting to gather information against Okamoto so that he could remove the latter from the camp, but at that time no one was willing to come forward. On February 14, Samuel Menin, a Denver attorney, arrived in camp to consult with the FPC concerning their stand and the expected outcome of a test case dealing with the legalities of applying Selective Service law to men held behind barbed wire. By organizing a test case and going to court over the draft question, the FPC believed that members might regain full citizenship rights for all Japanese Americans. [5]

Toward the end of February, Guy Robertson met with FBI special agent Harry McMillen to discuss the activities of Okamoto and the FPC. Robertson told McMillen that he had been trying to gather incriminating evidence against Okamoto and Paul Nakadate who, according to Robertson, was the number two man in the FPC. But despite his efforts, no incriminating evidence was collected. Robertson believed that if he could get someone in camp to state that the FPC was telling draftees not to report, he could have the group, or at least its leaders, tried for sedition. [6]

On February 28, the FPC sent a petition to President Roosevelt. The petition stated that Japanese Americans had gone along with the government relocation program, and after almost two years behind barbed wire, they felt that the status of their citizenship deserved clarification. A few of the requests were to be allowed to join branches of the service other than the army, to be allowed to return to their homes, to have government aid in abolishing anti-Japanese propaganda, and to have full restoration of their civil rights. [7] Filing the petition drew more attention to Okamoto and the FPC. But it was not sympathetic attention.

March was the high point of FPC influence at Heart Mountain. During the first week of the month, the group worked hard to present its views to the community. A circular went through the camp stating that it was the intention of the FPC and its followers to ignore orders from the Selective Service until all civil rights had been restored. During that period, twelve men refused to report for preinduction physicals. Their names were turned over to the FBI and the United States District Attorney. Later in the week, copies of *Rocky Shimpo*, a Japanese community newspaper edited by James Omura and published in Denver, arrived in camp with articles supporting the stand taken by the FPC. At that point, the situation appeared to be going well for the FPC.[8]

Near the end of March, Guy Robertson told Dillon Myer he feared that more men would refuse to abide by Selective Service orders. Robertson's concerns were well founded. During those last weeks of the month, sixteen more men refused to report for preinduction physicals. The first twelve men who refused to report to Cheyenne were arrested by U. S. Marshalls. As the number of resisters grew, the FPC came forward and made it clear that it did not want members whose only concern was avoiding the draft. The committee leadership said that evading the draft was not the purpose of the organization.[9]

By the first week of April, Robertson was in a state of panic. He had shipped Okamoto off to Tule Lake, and in so doing believed that he had solved his draft resister problems. But by that time, the number of those refusing to report for preinduction physicals had risen to fifty-four. Robertson felt that arresting the first twelve resisters would deter others, but he was wrong. The FPC continued to work hard, and in addition to the support it received from *Rocky Shimpo*, there was an outside group in Pasadena, California fighting for the restoration of rights for Japanese Americans (the identity of the Pasadena group is not given in Robertson's report). Their slogan was, "Justice Delayed is Justice Denied."[10] At that time, Robertson was also faced with the problem of what to do with the other forty-two draft resisters. The U. S. Attorney in Cheyenne was frantically trying to find space for them in various jails throughout Wyoming before issuing more arrest warrants.[11]

On April 3 and 4, Robertson held "leave clearance hearings" for Paul Nakadate, Ben Wakaye and Frank Emi. The term, "leave clearance hearings," might lead one to believe that these hearings had something to do with the men involved being able to leave the camp to work. In reality they were a frantic attempt by Guy Robertson to get one or all of the three men, all members of the FPC leadership, to incriminate themselves or others in acts of sedition. The questions asked in the interviews had nothing to do with leaving camp; they concerned the FPC and its members. Robertson seemed most obsessed with the location of the money that members paid to join the FPC ($2). But after hours of interrogation, he ended up with nothing. The transcripts of the interrogations were turned over to the FBI.[12]

By the middle of April, the other forty-two draft resisters had been arrested and were held on $2,000 bond in various jails throughout Wyoming. Samuel Menin, the Denver Attorney who agreed to defend the resisters, visited the men and encouraged them to accept their draft notices. Guy Robertson was less than appreciative of Menin's suggestion because he felt that a good number would accept and then be sent back to Heart Mountain until they were called. Once back in camp, Robertson believed the resisters would continue their anti-draft activities and said "... we will be bothered all through the summer ...." [13]

During the same time period in which Robertson was trying to gain control of the situation as far as the draft resisters were concerned, the government decided to send Nisei war hero, Ben Kuroki, on a three-camp public relations tour. Kuroki, a Nebraska farm boy who had never been interned, served as an aerial gunner on a B-24 bomber in thirty missions over Europe and North Africa. Kuroki's decorations included two Distinguished Flying Crosses and an Air Medal. Kuroki's visit was well received by some of the younger people in camp, but the Issei and many older Nisei felt that he was naive coming to Heart Mountain and trying to instill, or boost, the patriotic spirit. Since he had never been interned, some Heart Mountain residents took exception to the Kuroki tour. The tour of Heart Mountain, Topaz, and Minidoka was not the huge success the government had hoped for. [14] Kuroki soon left the states to fly twenty-eight more missions over Japan, while Robertson returned to the problem of dealing with the draft resisters.

Ben Kuroki with Guy Robertson at Heart Mountain (ERC).

Through the month of April, Robertson became more convinced that the stand he had taken and his efforts to root out the leaders of the FPC was the right choice. Even the ACLU (American Civil Liberties Union) advised the leader of the FPC, Kiyoshi Okamoto, that while the group had a good moral case, not reporting for the draft was a bad idea. Since Robertson could not get members of the FPC to incriminate themselves, he blamed most of his problems, the activities of the FPC, on *Rocky Shimpo*. He was delighted when he heard that the editor, James Omura, had been fired from his job. With Omura losing his job and the FPC leadership tucked away at Tule Lake, the situation was looking up, as far as Robertson was concerned. But by the first week in May, another group refused to report for preinduction physicals. That resulted in additional arrests and brought the total number to sixty-four resisters in custody of the Justice Department. One of the resisters was believed to be mentally deficient and was later released. A Federal Grand Jury was scheduled to meet soon to decide whether or not to indict the jailed members of the group. [15]

On May 8, 1944, the Grand Jury was convened in Cheyenne and brought indictments against the sixty-three Heart Mountain draft resisters. The charges, according to U. S. District Attorney Carl Sackett, were for failure to report to the local draft board in Powell. The resisters were represented by Samuel Menin of Denver and Clyde Watts of Cheyenne. In a pretrial motion, the defendants agreed to be tried as a group and waived a jury trial. The defendants in *The United States vs. Shigeru Fuji* (No. 4928 Criminal), were officially charged with violation of Section 311, Title 50, U.S.C.A. Selective Service and Training Act of 1940. The legal proceeding, which began at 10:00 a.m. on Monday, June 12, 1944, before District Judge T. Blake Kennedy, was the largest mass trial in Wyoming's history. [16]

Kennedy went over the trial agenda with the defendants so they would be aware of what was going on. Jack Tono, one of the defendants, said that some of the resisters felt they did not stand much chance when Kennedy referred to members of the group as, "You Jap Boys." [17] Tono said that Kennedy quickly corrected himself but had already shown what kind of a person they were dealing with. On the other hand, despite Kennedy's apparent prejudice, Mits Koshiyama and some of the other defendants believed in the system and thought that they would be acquitted. The trial had barely gotten underway when it was held up for nearly thirty minutes. One of the resisters was called to sit with his lawyers before the court but did not respond. After a short recess and conference between Menin and his clients, the group returned to the courtroom. The individual took his place with his attorneys. Menin explained that the name of the person in question was not being pronounced properly and he was not sure if he was the man being summoned. According to Tono, Menin advised all of the resisters to get similar haircuts, and Koshiyama said they were further directed not to answer when the judge called their names. Menin told the group that it was up to the court to prove the identity of each individual resister. Tono was not impressed with Menin's strategy. He said the group looked like a bunch of Buddhist monks, and that if the court wanted to identify the men individually all it had to do was have fingerprints taken. [18]

The trial got underway, and the prosecution began to present its case. Alta Christensen, the clerk for the Powell Draft Board, was the first witness called. She was on the stand all day June 12 and into June 13. Christensen stated that all of those named by the prosecution had been mailed draft notices. During cross examination, Menin said that the individual in question, Ken Sumida, was classified 4-C in California, and he asked Christensen if that did not mean that

Sumida was an enemy alien. When Christensen started to explain, Menin told her to answer "Yes" or "No." When she said she needed to explain, Judge Kennedy told her to answer "Yes" or "No" and then give her explanation. Menin objected and told the judge that he did not think the court had a right to interfere with the cross examination. Kennedy overruled Menin saying, "I don't care what you think . . . ." [19]

United States District Attorney Carl Sackett, a man who believed that resisting the draft was proof of disloyalty, next put four FBI agents on the stand. The agents testified that all sixty-three of the defendants were willing to serve in the armed forces if their constitutional rights were restored. Under cross examination, Menin brought out the fact that at least one of the defendants tried to join the army while in California and was refused enlistment. When asked, all of the agents also said that they believed each of the defendants to be a loyal American. [20]

On June 26, 1944, Judge Kennedy handed down his decision. He said that the legality of removal or relocation of Japanese Americans from their homes on the West Coast had not been ruled on by the courts (that decision did not come down until December of 1944 in the Endo case). Kennedy believed that since the Supreme Court found that it was legal to put a curfew on people of Japanese ancestry on the West Coast (*Minoru Yasui vs. the United States*), it was, in his opinion, probably also legal to remove those people if the government chose to. He also said that the defense maintained that there was no criminal intent on the part of the defendants. According to Kennedy, refusal to obey the draft board showed willful intent to violate the law. Addressing the claim that the defendants would comply with draft laws when their citizenship was restored, Kennedy said the Selective Service classification of 1-A meant that their citizenship had been established beyond a shadow of a doubt. It was Kennedy's personal feeling that,

> If they are truly loyal American citizens they should, at least when they have been recognized as such, embrace the opportunity to discharge the duties of citizens by offering themselves in the cause of our National defense. [21]

After conveying to the defendants his explanations and personal points of view, Kennedy found all sixty-three men guilty and sentenced them to three years in prison. He added, after adjournment, that it was also his opinion that the sixty-three would rather sit in prison than serve their country. [22]

Kennedy's decision was appealed, but the higher courts refused to entertain arguments that the constitutional rights of the defendants had been violated. The conclusions of the higher courts were based on a technical interpretation of the law, and they upheld the Kennedy decision. Thirty of the older men, those above the age of twenty-five, were sent to serve their sentence in the federal penitentiary at Fort Leavenworth, Kansas. The other thirty-three, who were under the age of twenty-five, were sent to the federal prison at McNeil Island in Washington. After serving one year of their terms, the resisters came up for parole. A guard at McNeil Island told Jack Tono, "Oh, hell, you guys are clean as a whistle, no record. If you don't get paroled, there's something wrong." [23] However, parole was denied. Dillon Myer sent a letter to Edward Ennis of the Justice Department and informed him that he (Myer) did not want the resisters paroled because he felt it would be a bad influence on other internees who might have considered resisting the draft. Ennis informed James Bennet at the Bureau of Prisons that draft resisters could not be paroled until Dillon Myer was first consulted. [24]

While some of the defendants expected to be found guilty, they were enraged with the workings of the judicial system. In a similar trial held for a group of draft resisters from Tule Lake, U. S. District Judge Louis Goodman granted a motion to dismiss the charges against that group. As with the Heart Mountain resisters, the Tule Lake group claimed that their constitutional rights had been denied them, and when returned, they would serve in the armed forces. Judge Goodman said that those who were incarcerated in the relocation center at Tule Lake were not free agents, and the decisions or pleas they made were therefore not free and voluntary. He concluded by saying,

> It is shocking to the conscience, that an American citizen be confined on the ground of disloyalty and then, while so under duress and restraint, be compelled to serve in the armed forces or be prosecuted for not yielding to such compulsion. [25]

The case at Tule Lake was dismissed, and the defendants returned to the camp. In Arizona, approximately one-hundred draft resisters from the Poston Relocation Center were tried and found guilty. However, the judge in that case did not hand down jail sentences. Instead, he fined each defendant one penny. [26]

On December 23, 1947, Harry S. Truman signed Presidential Proclamation 2762. That proclamation granted a full pardon to the Nisei draft resisters, and their records were wiped clean. Truman said that while he recognized the importance of the draft in the defense of the nation, he also understood the situation the Nisei were in. The President said he appreciated the resisters' feelings and their reaction to orders sent out by local draft boards. Their resentment toward removal from their homes and being classified as undesirables was understandable, he said. [27]

The conviction of the sixty-three draft resisters was not the end of the FPC. A smaller group of resisters from Heart Mountain was also tried and convicted, and in late July, 1944, the seven leaders of the FPC were arrested on charges of conspiracy. Some of the men were arrested at Heart Mountain; others, like Okamoto, whom Guy Robertson had sent to Tule Lake, were arrested there. In addition to these men, James Omura, the former editor of *Rocky Shimpo*, was also arrested on charges of conspiracy for the articles he had written in support of the FPC. [28]

In a hearing on August 5 before Federal District Judge Eugene Rice, defense attorney A. L. Wirin tried to have the case dismissed because the defendants had been placed in camps without "due process." Like Judge Kennedy in the resisters' trial, Rice said that that was not the issue in the charges in question. The motion was denied. Seven of the eight men were eventually found guilty of conspiring to evade the draft. James Omura was "cleared on grounds of freedom of the press." Despite the verdict, Omura was ostracized by, or isolated himself from, the Japanese American community for nearly forty years. Of those found guilty, two, Minoru Tamesa and Ben Wakaye, each serving a three-year term for draft evasion, had two years added to their sentences. Guntaro Kubota received two years. Isamu Horino, Frank Emi, Paul Nakadate and Kiyoshi Okamoto were each sentenced to four years in prison. [29]

> Attorney A. L. Wirin appealed Judge Rice's decision to the Tenth Circuit Court of Appeals. Judge Bratton overturned the Rice decision writing; In respect to the issue as to whether the appellants with honesty of purpose and innocence of motive in a good faith effort to bring about a test case to determine their exempt status under the Selective Service Act, Judge Rice had erred by not considering the right of American citizens to question or to refuse to comply with laws they considered unconstitutional. [30]

Although the legality of drafting Japanese Americans from the camps was never addressed, the FPC was exonerated with the Bratton decision.

These men stood up and fought for their rights as American citizens at a time when it was not popular to do so. Mits Koshiyama, one of the Heart Mountain sixty-three, said that when confronted with the decision of whether to report for a preinduction physical he asked himself, "if a person is going to fight for freedom and democracy, shouldn't he be enjoying the same rights he is entrusted to defend?" [31] Koshiyama had three brothers who served in the armed forces. They respected his decision and he respected theirs. [32]

Jack Tono was another of the Heart Mountain draft resisters. He, like the others, said he would gladly have fought America's enemies once his rights and those of his family were restored. Tono said the resisters were looking for a clarification of their citizenship status. They were tired of being part-time citizens. In one instance they were seen as a threat to national security and locked behind barbed wire, but while still incarcerated, they were told that as citizens they were required to serve in the army. It was that part-time citizen and part-time alien situation that Tono, Koshiyama, and the others were appealing to the government to address. [33]

Tono and Koshiyama said it was bad enough that they had to stand and fight against their own government, but they were also opposed by their own leaders. The JACL (Japanese American Citizens League) not only did not support the FPC and the draft resisters, it also spoke out openly against the stand they took. [34] Wayne Collins, a San Francisco attorney working on the Korematsu case (a case testing the legality of Japanese evacuation) said, "The JACL pretended to be the spokesmen for all Japanese Americans but they wouldn't stand up for their people." [35] He also said that the JACL, "led their people like a bunch of goddam doves to the concentration camps." [36]

When the draft resisters stood up for their rights, they stood alone. It took the passing of the "Free Speech" movement at Berkeley, Vietnam war protests, and the civil disobedience of Martin Luther King Jr. in the 1960's, before many Americans appreciated the stand taken by the Heart Mountain draft resisters. Yet even today, this issue divides many within the Japanese American community.

While Guy Robertson was addressing issues inside the camp, he was also engaged in a running battle with a very vocal minority of local individuals who called for restricting Heart Mountain residents to the camp.

Chapter XIII

Powell and Cody: Efforts to Exclude the Japanese

John Nelson, WRA official at Heart Mountain, stated that toward the end of December, 1942, he noticed a distinct change in the attitude of people in Powell and Cody toward the camp. It must be pointed out that this attitude was that of a very vocal minority. Nelson said locals viewed the Japanese as great people when they were working in the fields, but once the crops were in and their labor no longer needed, the locals had no use for them. That attitude was particularly prevalent among the political leaders of the two towns and some of the "upper class" business people.[1]

On April 24, 1943, in the midst of the *Denver Post*'s investigation of Heart Mountain, a joint meeting of the town councils of Powell and Cody was held at the Town Hall in Cody. Attending from Powell was Mayor Ora Bever and Councilmen Ed Althoff, Dick Jones, and Elvin Royer. Attending from Cody was Mayor Paul Stock and Councilmen Roy Holm, Raymond Howe, Paul Sweitzer and T. F. Trimmer. The two mayors had also requested that Heart Mountain Director Guy Robertson be present. The meeting was called to discuss the "problem" of controlling the Japanese who were visiting Powell and Cody and being allowed to wander around the two towns at will. The two councils were concerned most with the Japanese purchasing rationed commodities and intoxicating liquor.[2]

After an extensive discussion, the members of the two councils decided that the Japanese should not be allowed into Powell or Cody unless they were on business and were properly supervised. When Guy Robertson arrived, the issues were again discussed. Robertson assured the town councils that if they stated in writing that they did not want any Japanese in their towns, he would do everything in his power to comply with their wishes. Robertson then excused himself and returned to Heart Mountain. In the meantime, the councils adopted a formal statement of exclusion. The men agreed that no indefinite passes should be issued to Japanese to visit or work in either community. They felt that visitor passes should be issued only to the soldiers from the camp. However, the councilmen did not want these restrictions to interfere in any way with the employment of the Japanese in work "essential to the war effort, particularly necessary labor on ranches and farms."[3]

On May 3 at the regular meeting of the Powell Town Council, the resolution outlined by the joint Powell and Cody councils was brought up for a vote. Ed Althoff made a motion that the resolution be passed. The motion was seconded by Dick Jones and passed unanimously by the other members of the council. In Cody, the Town Council was also meeting on May 3. Mayor Paul Stock reported to the Cody group that he had been informed by Mayor Bever of Powell that the exclusion

121

resolution was passed in that town. Stock called for a vote and the resolution was also passed unanimously by the Cody council. After the Cody group had adopted the resolution to keep the Japanese out of town, the Cody Club (Chamber of Commerce) and the Cody Lions Club asked the council if they could use the town's auditorium to entertain the Caucasian personnel who worked at Heart Mountain. The two groups felt that they should extend a welcome to those people. A copy of the resolution was sent to Guy Robertson at Heart Mountain, Governor Lester Hunt, and each member of Wyoming's congressional delegation. [4]

On May 6, shortly after finding out about the exclusion resolution, Powell merchants protested the actions taken by Mayor Bever and the town council, but the complaint had no immediate effect. Upon receiving his copy of the resolution, Guy Robertson sent a copy to WRA Director Dillon Myer. The two men decided to stop issuing passes of any kind allowing internees to visit Powell or Cody. Those out on leave were allowed to stay out for the time being, but the WRA was considering the removal of Park County from its approved list of places for internees to work. If Park County was removed from the list, those on leave at that time would be recalled to the camp. [5]

A short time after the WRA took its stand on the further issuing of passes in Park County, Joe Carroll, Heart Mountain's Employment Chief, was invited to speak in Powell. Carroll was asked by the Powell Club (Chamber of Commerce) to discuss the Japanese "problem." He told the group of thirty local businessmen that the WRA had canceled all leaves, as requested by Powell and Cody town officials. Carroll said that some people in the two communities might have believed that the cancellation of passes was aimed at harming the two towns, but he assured them that it was not. The action was taken by the WRA office in Washington in an effort to get along with the two communities and do as they asked. Carroll asked his audience, "Just what do you want, . . . ?" [6] He told them that they could not expect the internees to go out and help area farmers with their crops when they were not even allowed on the streets of the communities. Carroll assured those in attendance that no more passes would be issued unless the two towns showed a favorable sentiment. [7]

On July 15, the Powell and Cody Town Councils again met in joint session. Under pressure from area farmers and ranchers, the two councils adopted a supplement to the original resolution. However, the second resolution did not rescind the first. The group said that their original resolution in no way reflected the views of people residing outside the two communities. They stated that it was never their intention to interfere with the employment of Japanese on farms and ranches within the county. The two councils also explained that due to the WRA's interpretation of the first resolution, the farmers and ranchers in Park County were "unjustly being deprived access to the petential [sic] labor supply now existing at the Heart Mountain Relocation Center, . . ." [8] The two councils felt that the required labor should be released and "recommended" that Guy Robertson furnish records

122

of all available labor to the War Labor Board. [9]

Even though the second resolution passed by Powell and Cody politicians conceded nothing, leave and visitor passes were once again issued to internees to go out and work for area farmers and others. By August, the American Legion in Powell was converting part of its building into a barracks so that up to 170 laborers from Heart Mountain would have a place to eat and sleep. The purpose of the project was to enable area farmers to drop off laborers in town as opposed to driving them back to Heart Mountain every night. It also gave laborers access to stores in town. The project was a great success, and thanks were given to WRA officials, Wyoming Agricultural Extension Service and the U. S. Employment Service. [10] Thanks to the laborers seemed to be missing. During late September, the Powell area was pleading for laborers. Eighty-five men were staying at the dormitory set up by the American Legion. They were being paid sixty-five cents per hour and charged one dollar and fifty cents per day for meals and housing. The men appeared to be satisfied with the situation. The problem was that an additional fifty workers were needed immediately in order to "save the $3,000,000 bean crop in the Powell Valley." [11] Twenty-four men were needed at the bean mill, owned by Mayor Ora Bever, and at least twenty-five on the farms. John McElroy, speaking for Powell farmers, said that the labor "must be made available immediately or a large portion of the crop will be lost because there is no other source of manpower." [12]

By the first week of November, the crops were in and the potential disaster had been avoided. There was at that time no longer any need for labor from Heart Mountain, and the Powell Town Council was once again looking to cut off all visitor passes. At the November 5 council meeting, the Japanese "problem" was the major point of discussion. Seven of Powell's businessmen attended the meeting and asked that no action be taken against the residents of Heart Mountain. In addition, a number of Powell businessmen also sent letters to the council. Melvin Evans told the mayor and council members that people from Heart Mountain who were allowed to come to town on passes had never been a nuisance or caused any trouble. Evans said he would back any group that opposed the action against the Japanese which was being contemplated. Al Fryer asked that no more resolutions be passed concerning the Japanese in Park County. Fryer said that ninety-five percent of the businesses in town opposed any action against the internees and pointed out that the council was "supposed" to represent the wishes of all the people in Powell and not just their own prejudices. The council adjourned and took no action at that time. [13]

At the next meeting in Powell, Councilman Dick Jones stated that a letter should be sent to Guy Robertson at Heart Mountain to let him know of the council's sentiments concerning the Japanese "problem." A letter was drafted explaining to Robertson that he needed to be made aware of the "true" situation in Powell. The councilmen said they were simply trying to avoid any trouble that might arise as a result of the Japanese being present in town. They were concerned that with the growing number of casualties in the Pacific Theater, there might be more "incidents" like the one that had recently taken place. The council said it would be in everyone's best interest if passes were curtailed, and that all Japanese living in and around Powell should be sent back to the camp since there was no longer an agricultural labor shortage. [14]

The "incident" to which the Powell Council made reference in its letter to Robertson took place at the Jim Hart farm near Garland in late October. There, A. H. Petrich tried to run down five internees with his car. The men were working for Hart and were crossing the highway from one field to another when Petrich swerved at them. When the men dove into the barrow ditch, Petrich stopped and told them he would be back later, and that he was going to kill the workers. Petrich soon returned with a friend, Dale Wirth. The men were threatening the internees with a gun when Hart heard the disturbance and ran to the scene. Hart hit Petrich and knocked him out. Dale Wirth took a swing, with whiskey bottle, at Murl Peterson, who also worked for Hart. Wirth was soon overpowered. The police were summoned, and arrested both men. Wirth was fined $15 for disturbing the peace. Petrich appeared before a Powell judge in justice court. He was fined $125 and sentenced to sixty days in jail. The Powell judge then promptly suspended the fine and jail sentence. [15]

In contrast to the efforts of Powell's political leaders, the Cody Town Council never discussed the Japanese "problem" following the second joint resolution. Those holding an anti-Japanese view in Cody made their feelings known through the rantings of Senator E. V. Robertson and the on-again, off-again, anti-Heart Mountain sentiments of Milward Simpson. In addition, a number of Cody businesses posted, "No Japs Allowed" signs in their storefront windows. [16] But the Powell Town Council, led by Ora Bever and Dick Jones, was bound and determined that no Japanese people be allowed in town except during labor shortages.

The Powell Council tried to use the incident at the Hart farm to illustrate the sentiment in Park County and show why the Japanese should not be allowed in town. In truth, it was the only such incident in Powell during the entire existence of the camp. There was also one incident in Cody. In that town, an internee was strolling down the street when one of the MP's from the camp walked up and hit him. The internee suffered a broken jaw. The entire group of MP's was shipped out the next day (not because of that incident) and no action was taken against the soldier. [17] In the three-year and three-month existence of the camp, these were the only two incidents which could have been used to support the contentions of the Powell Town Council that there was a Japanese "problem."

The Powell politicians left the issue alone for nearly six months, until June of 1944. At the June 5 regular meeting of the council, the big topic of discussion was the large number of Heart Mountain residents on the streets of Powell. At that time all of the councilmen, and the mayor, voted to once again send letters to both of Wyoming's U. S. Senators, Governor Hunt, Congressman Barrett and Secretary of the Interior Harold Ickes. The letters were all different and explained different problems to the individual political leaders. Each letter was signed by Mayor Bever and four councilmen. [18]

Council members informed Secretary Ickes that the Registrar of Voters in San Francisco stated that internees were still legal residents of the areas from which they were removed. The Powell group wanted to know when the internees would be sent back to their residences and asked that someone in authority promise them that the Japanese would be removed in the near future. Council members explained that Park County was sparsely populated and said if the Japanese were allowed to remain they could damage the area's economy, though they did not say how. In closing, council members said they just did not want the Japanese in Park County. [19]

The message to Governor Hunt was somewhat different. The council informed Hunt that Powell and the State of Wyoming were faced with a serious problem, the Japanese at Heart Mountain. The position taken, according to the group, had the support of the entire community. They did not want the Japanese left in the area after the war, nor did they want them to be allowed to "continue to run at large in and out of the town of Powell as they were doing at this time." [20]

At Heart Mountain, Guy Robertson was told by the Powell Council that the Japanese were allowed into the state only because Wyomingites were assured they would be strictly confined. According to the council, there were at that time thirty-four evacuees living in Powell (domestic help) and only Laramie had more. The group explained that its members did not want any Japanese from the camp living in town. They told Robertson that for the safety of those who lived in Powell and the Japanese themselves, and as a show of respect for the town's servicemen fighting in the war, the council wanted an end to the issuing of visitor passes for internee trips to Powell. [21]

During the middle of June, Guy Robertson heard from a number of the Powell businessmen concerning the issue. T. T. Dodson, President of the Powell Club, invited Robertson to speak at the club's next meeting to outline what he planned to do about the demands of the Powell Town Council. Melvin Evans also contacted Robertson and informed him that most people in Powell had no idea what the council members were doing until after they had done it. He said it was unfortunate that the mayor was such a determined "hot-head." Al Fryer informed Robertson that he and most of the merchants in town hoped that the camp director would simply disregard the demands of the Powell Council because they did not represent the views of the entire community as they claimed. [22]

Guy Robertson and Joe Carroll both attended the meeting of the Powell Club on June 19. Robertson told the group to let him know if they were not satisfied with his program of letting Heart Mountain residents travel to Powell to shop on occasion. If it was the will of the community, he would stop issuing all passes. Robertson did not feel it was right that Powell people were willing to let Japanese Americans fight and die in the war and then not allow them or their parents to shop in Powell stores. Following Robertson's talk, the thirty-five who had gathered for the meeting discussed what action, if any, they thought should be taken. The group reached a consensus on one point. Members felt that Ora Bever, as mayor of Powell, did not have the power to restrict anyone from town simply on the basis of race or color. [23]

Some of the merchants also contacted Governor Hunt to make him aware of their feelings. Al Fryer informed the governor that Powell's anti-Heart Mountain mayor and his town council were trying to cause trouble again for the Japanese Americans. He also said that if the FBI and the War Department felt that these people were "all right," then Powell town officials had over stepped their bounds with the actions they were trying to implement. Upon receipt of Fryer's letter, Hunt informed Bever that he had received a number of similar messages and suggested that the mayor "let the matter rest . . . ." [24]

Bever also received a letter from Dillon Myer on the subject of camp closures following the war. Myer assured the mayor that the WRA was going to close all of the camps when the war ended. However, Myer pointed out to Bever that once the war was over, Japanese Americans were free to live anywhere they chose to. He added that the mayor had no business even questioning such rights. At the next town council meeting, Bever told Guy Robertson that he would allow a small number of visitors from the camp into Powell under certain conditions. The main condition was that Robertson get a statement in writing which guaranteed that all Japanese would be removed from the area following the war. Robertson said he would do what he could. [25]

Within a month of the June council meeting Bever wrote to the governor informing Hunt of the discussion with Guy Robertson. "The people" of the community would be tolerant and let a few Japanese into town once a written statement was received saying that all Japanese would be removed from the area, and the state, after the war. Unless Bever received such a statement "the authorities [sic] of Powell will remove any and all Japanese coming into the city from the Heart Mountain Center on visiting passes." [26] Bever told Hunt that the WRA said it intended to close all camps following the war, and added, "We are not interested in what the authorities intentions are, we are interested in what will be done." [27] Bever also informed the governor that as mayor, he was apprising Hunt of "the true facts surrounding the Jap problem here and the wishes of the people in this country." [28] Bever told Hunt in no uncertain terms, that until he received a statement saying the Japanese would be removed after the war he expected the governor to do everything in his power to cut off all passes from Heart Mountain to Powell. [29]

Guy Robertson informed the governor that Joe Carroll spent ten days in Powell interviewing residents of that community. The vast majority did not care that Heart Mountain residents were allowed to come to town. Another meeting was held with the merchants in Powell, and all of those in attendance wanted Robertson to let visitors leave the camp to do their shopping. The survey by Carroll and the meeting with Powell merchants made it clear that the stand which Bever and the town council had taken against the Japanese was their own. According to Robertson it did not have the backing of the entire community as the mayor claimed. Robertson felt things would work themselves out but was afraid that a major confrontation was brewing between the merchants and town council. [30]

On August 8, Hunt informed Mayor Bever and the Powell Town Council that he had received a great deal of mail from people in and around Powell who took a different view of the Japanese problem, and he said that he could not ignore it. The governor said he would take no action against the relocation center at that time. Instead he decided to send a private investigator to Powell to see what the real situation was. Upon receiving the governor's letter, Bever said he welcomed an investigation and assured Hunt that the findings would support everything the mayor and council were saying. The governor explained to Bever that the investigator would be in Powell toward the end of August and would not let his identity be known to anyone. [31]

William Bradley, a Wyoming Highway Patrol Captain, was the man Governor Hunt sent to Powell as an undercover investigator. Bradley reported to the governor that he had surveyed a good cross section of the town's population. Approximately sixty-five percent of those whom he interviewed (the interviews were carried out in a "passing the time of day" type conversation) had no objection to the internees at Heart Mountain traveling to Powell to shop. Most residents said they did not care one way or the other. Some said they did not care for the Japanese, but since they were American citizens felt they should be able to do what they wanted. Bradley also noticed that some of the Heart Mountain evacuees were working as domestics and in some of the laundries in town. Over all, he said, a majority of the community's citizens believed that passes should be issued for visits to Powell. [32]

Hunt sent a copy of the Bradley report to Bever. He told the mayor the in light of the report and the many other letters from people in Powell, the opinions of Bever and the council were not those of the community in general. The governor suggested to Bever that "it would be best to let well enough alone." [33] The mayor never raised the issue again. It has been suggested that Bever's attitude toward the Japanese was shaped by the fact that he lost a son in the Pacific Theater. While the Bevers' family loss may have contributed to the mayor's anti-Japanese sentiments, his feelings were made very clear only sixty days after Pearl Harbor in a telegram to then governor Nels Smith. In that message Bever said he supported Smith's stand on keeping the "Japs" out of Wyoming.

A year after Mayor Bever had dropped the issue of allowing the Japanese to shop in Powell, a new group from that town began to attack Heart Mountain and its residents. That organization was the Powell chapter of "American War Dads." The members of the group contacted Lester Hunt and WRA Director Myer. The main concern of the Powell War Dads was that all Japanese at Heart Mountain be removed from Wyoming. The group felt that the $25 relocation grant was not enough money to insure that the Japanese could make it out of the state (The WRA gave each internee $25 in expense money once he or she was discharged from the camp). The reason the War Dads wanted the Japanese out of the state, and out of the county in particular, was because they felt that since their sons were fighting and dying for their country, those who made it back should be rewarded for their service. The group wanted the Heart Mountain Reclamation Project opened for homesteading and felt that veterans should be given preference in the homestead acquisition process. [34]

When Guy Robertson received a copy of the demands, or concerns, of the Powell War Dads from Governor Hunt, he immediately pointed out that there were 758 men from Heart Mountain who fought in Europe and the Pacific which meant that there were more "war dads" at Heart Mountain than there were in Powell. Robertson added that the Japanese Americans were also fighting and dying for their country and that many were members of the 442nd, the most decorated unit in the army. Dillon Myer, after hearing of the demands made by the Powell War Dads, said that the decision in the Endo case made it clear that the people at Heart Mountain could live anywhere they wanted to. Neither Robertson or Myer really cared what the Powell War Dads wanted. The two men had been presenting the same facts to the public, and particularly to groups from Powell and Cody, for more than three years. [35]

Myer and Robertson had presented the facts time and time again, and they were ignored time and time again by apparent racist individuals who were only concerned with their own selfish motives. As the Bradley report showed, the majority of the citizens in Powell did not show much concern with the large Japanese population at Heart Mountain. This can be credited largely to the Mary Oyama and John Kitasako columns published in the *Powell Tribune*. Both writers endeared themselves to Powell residents and portrayed Heart Mountain as just another community in Park County. It was a very vocal, self-serving minority that continually caused problems for everyone concerned and led, wrongly, to the belief by many internees that a majority of the people in Powell and Cody were prejudiced against them. Once again, the silence of the majority, was often seen as tacit approval of the actions of a few.

Chapter XIV

Closing the Camp

By the fall of 1944, the war was going well for the allies. Hitler was on the run in Europe and even though the fighting was fierce and bloody in the Pacific, Japan was losing ground. The end of the war was in sight, but it was still a ways off. A major political point of concern was what to do with the Japanese and Japanese Americans who were still in internment camps and relocation centers. Most of the evacuees had been removed from California, and politicians in that state, for the most part, did not want them back. Senator Downey of California was proposing a national, "share the Japs program." [1] Downey and other politicians from California were saying that the Japanese should be spread evenly throughout the United States. [2]

Political motives were the main reason that people of Japanese ancestry were still behind barbed wire during the autumn of 1944. As early as May of that year. Secretary of War, Henry Stimson, told President Roosevelt that there was no longer any military reason to keep Japanese people away from the West Coast. Roosevelt said that he could not review the issue until his Cabinet met later in the year. Allowing the Japanese to return to the coast was still a very hot political issue in California and, conveniently, the President's Cabinet did not meet until after the election in November. [3] Roosevelt was more concerned with winning California's electoral votes in November than he was with the welfare of a small minority group.

The Executive Branch of the Government put the issue on hold, but the Judicial Branch was about to apply pressure. On October 11, 1944, the Supreme Court met to decide the Korematsu and Endo cases. Fred Korematsu had undergone plastic surgery in an effort to evade evacuation and remain on the West Coast. The Korematsu case was challenging the legality of the evacuation. Mitsuye Endo was discharged from her job on the basis of her race, and then confined, first to an assembly center and then to a relocation center. Endo's attorney, James Purcell, was challenging the legality of confining a loyal American citizen against his or her will. It was Purcell's contention that Endo could be detained or interned only long enough to establish her loyalty. He also said that neither the President nor Congress had given the WRA any power to confine Japanese Americans or anyone else. If such authority had been given, it would have been a violation of the constitutional rights of those interned. By the autumn of 1944, Endo had already pledged her loyalty to the United States, but she was still being held in a relocation center in Utah. She had been detained for two and one-half years when her case went before the Supreme Court. [4]

On October 16, 1944 the Supreme Court met and decided the two cases.

Although the decision went against Korematsu, and the evacuation was found to be legal, the Court said that the WRA had no authority to hold Endo or any other Japanese Americans against their will once they were found to be loyal to the United States. Justice William O. Douglas wrote the decision in the Endo case. Douglas was ready to present the opinion publicly on December 4 but was under pressure from Chief Justice Stone to hold off. The White House was aware of the decision before it was announced publicly and used that knowledge to its advantage. It was decided that the opinion in the Endo case would be given on Monday, December 18. With the White House aware of the decision in *Ex Parte Endo*, the War Department issued a press release on December 17 announcing that Japanese and Japanese Americans who were loyal to the United States were free to return to the West Coast. The following day the opinion in the Endo case was given, but it received very little press. In a unanimous decision, the Court stated "that the WRA had no statutory authority to detain Endo or other Japanese Americans whose loyalty had been certified." [5]

As early as November of 1944, rumors circulated through Heart Mountain that the camp would be closing. In early December, California Governor Earl Warren must have suspected the coming decision to end exclusion on the West Coast. He told newspaper reporters that his state would welcome the Japanese Americans back just as patriotically as it supported their removal. One would think that with the rumors of the camp closing, Governor Warren's statement, and the eventual designation of "X-DAY," the official end of exclusion from the West Coast, that the residents of Heart Mountain would have been overjoyed and making plans to return home. That was hardly the case. [6]

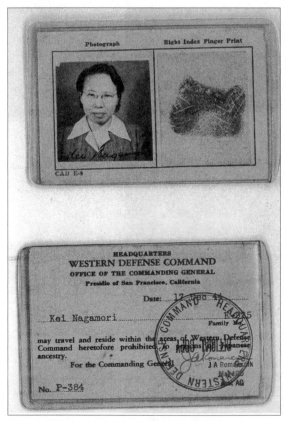

When returning to the West Coast, former internees were required to carry an identification card (JTIC).

Closing the Camp

Shortly following the announcement of "X-DAY," the WRA reported that it would begin a gradual closing of all camps. Not only were most internees not excited about being able to return to the coast, they were upset with the announcement that the camps would close. By December 1944, most of those who were going to relocate had already done so. The population of Heart Mountain was made up mostly of the very young and their mothers, and the very old. The youngsters would not finish the school year until June of 1945 and the elderly had, for the most part, lost everything they worked for and were not looking forward to starting over at an advanced age. By the end of December, only twelve families had made plans to return to the West Coast. In an effort to find out what the internee feeling was, A. T. Hansen, the WRA's Heart Mountain Community Analyst, surveyed a cross section of the residents. [7]

Hansen received a number of different responses when he asked internees why they were not leaving the camp immediately. One man in his fifties said he had been wiped out by the relocation process. He had lost his business and was forced to spend nearly $3,000 of his savings while he was at Heart Mountain, mostly on clothes for his children. His savings were gone. The man explained that he could not support his family washing dishes, and that was about the only type of work being offered to people of Japanese ancestry. [8]

During the war, relocation centers and internment camps were occasionally visited by the Spanish Consul. As a neutral country, Spain's representatives were allowed into the United States. The Spanish government served as a go-between and often worked as a sort of "Red Cross" relaying requests and information from Japanese citizens in the United States to the Japanese Government. When it was announced that the camps would close, some of the Issei, who were ineligible for United States citizenship and therefore, technically, citizens of Japan, wanted to send letters of protest to government officials in Washington D. C. and the Japanese government explaining the unfair treatment they were receiving. The Issei explained to both governments that they were forcibly uprooted from their homes and, in most instances, lost everything they had spent a lifetime working for when they were evacuated and interned. They were then told that they had to vacate the camp as it would soon be closed, with the WRA not caring if internees had a home to return to or not. The Spanish Consul delivered the letters of protest, but to no avail. [9]

A number of the internees wanted to stay in camp until the war was over. They felt that it might be possible to obtain better jobs when the war ended because anti-Japanese sentiment would not be so strong. Some of those who had nothing to go back to did not want to believe that the camps would close. They felt as one resident did. He said of the camp, "It's just like a town. You can't close a town." [10] The internees believed that since it was the government which caused them to lose everything, it was up to the government to take care of them. Guy Robertson and the other WRA administrators saw the situation in a different light. They were government bureaucrats who did what their superiors told them, and few showed much concern with the future of the internees. In the end, Robertson showed more concern for the civil servants working for him, than he did for the well being of Heart Mountain's residents. Mrs. Serisawa, with no home to return to, had her belongings packed for her and was physically forced onto the last train when the camp closed. Robertson referred to her as a "crackpot," while lamenting the fact that his employees might not be able to carry on with civil service careers because positions could not be found for them in other areas. [11]

By January 1945, Robertson decided that no visitors would be allowed into the camp. A number of evacuees who had relocated within the Rocky Mountain region visited the camp on occasion. Some who relocated and lost jobs returned to the camp for a visit and then stayed. A few of the Heart Mountain residents had Caucasian friends on the outside who would occasionally stop by to visit, but they were not allowed to enter the camp either. Robertson felt that if the camp was going to be closed, he had to keep visitors out so that the internees would not feel too much at home. Therefore, he believed that one way to compel the internees to leave camp after "X-DAY," was to cut off all visiting. Once visits from those on the outside were ended, Robertson told Myer that the residents became very antagonistic toward the WRA. The school was vandalized, and one evacuee who worked for internal security was beaten by four men. Any resident connected with the camp administration was seen as an informer or traitor, according to Robertson. [12]

Evacuees from all of the relocation centers were planning a conference in Salt Lake City to discuss the closing of the camps. Robertson told Myer that he felt Heart Mountain and all of the other camps should send delegations to the conference. But he also suggested that Myer attend to inform the evacuees that the liquidation process would continue no matter what. Robertson feared that the delegates would "meet and submit proposals that will be preposterous . . . ." The conference was held, and Myer did attend. Some delegates wanted to leave at least one camp open indefinitely so that people would have a place to stay as it would probably take some evacuees more time to find a place to relocate to. Myer refused. He informed those attending the conference that all camps would be closed by January 2, 1946. The delegates also asked Myer to consider some of the other requests they had. Upon their discharge from camp, internees wanted more than $25 and travel fare, which was what the WRA was giving at the time. Delegates also asked for long-term low-interest federal loans to help farmers to get reestablished. Since the farmers had lost everything on account of government policy, they felt that the government could at least loan them the money to get back on their feet. [13] In the end, the residents still received only $25 and transportation, and no loans.

In February 1945, one of the mess halls in camp was closed. That, to many residents, was a sign that the camp closing was a reality. The slow and gradual shut down of the camp made the issues of farm loans and insufficient expense money more important. Early on, residents had been concerned with the anti-Japanese sentiment back in California. By the end of February, however, they were more concerned with the economic problems of resettlement. One resident, who still had title to his land, visited his farm in the Santa Clara Valley. He said that while he had been accepted by the public, there was no land available for other returning farmers to rent. Many of those still in camp were Issei farmers who had to rent land in order to start over. Reports like that made by the internee from the Santa Clara Valley pushed economic concerns to the top of the list. In a poll taken of 4,000 Heart Mountain residents near the end of February, only nine percent said they could relocate under the existing policy and conditions. [14]

Closing the camp had other implications which not only affected the evacuees at Heart Mountain, but also some of the Caucasian residents of the Powell and Cody area. It was decided in early March that the camp's farming project would be abandoned. Since the WRA was trying to relocate all of the residents, there would not be sufficient manpower to operate the farm. The camp's agricultural project itself was developed in an effort to make the camp as self sufficient as possible. The farm was located within the 42,000 acres of the Heart Mountain Reclamation Project which had been set aside for use by the WRA. Before farming was begun, there was a great deal of work that had to be completed using WRA money and internee labor. [15]

Internees look on as water is turned into the canal (ERC).

When the camp was occupied, only the upper half of the main irrigation canal had been completed, and when tested, it leaked badly. Heart Mountain internees constructed more than 5,000 feet of the canal and waterproofed the other sections that leaked. Approximately 850 tons of bentonite was used in the waterproofing process. The canal was deemed ready for the 1943 growing season. Following the laborious process of clearing the sagebrush, the land was plowed and crops planted. All that was done in spite of local farmers' opinions that the canal could not be completed in time, and that crops would be planted too late in the year to produce any significant yield. The farming program was carried out under the watchful eyes of internees, James Ito, who held a degree in agriculture from the University of California at Berkeley, and Eiichi Edward Sakauye, who had worked for the County Agricultural Commissioner in San Jose, California prior to evacuation. When the crops were harvested in the autumn of 1943, the yield was more than 1,065 tons of produce, which went to help feed residents of the camp. The following year the yield more than doubled to 2,500 tons with a value of $135,413. The farm project also consisted of hog, chicken and cattle operations. [16]

Heart Mountain farm project shortly after planting (ERC).

The livestock portion of the camp's agricultural project became an important source of meat and eggs for Heart Mountain residents. Many thousands of animals were raised as part of the program. With so much livestock, the WRA felt it was necessary to have a full-time veterinarian on hand. That job was given to Dr. Minol Ota. Though a Japanese American, Ota was not an internee. After graduating from Texas A & M in June of 1942, Ota went to stay with his sister and brother-in-law, who lived in Powell, Wyoming. Ota stayed around Powell while the camp was being constructed and was eventually hired by WRA. Ota worked with internees and camp officials in caring for the livestock. On one occasion, the camp administration ordered that a census of the Heart Mountain chicken population be taken. The census revealed that nearly 2,000 chickens were missing. Doctor Ota explained that the chickens died of "barracks sickness." He said the disease was always fatal. Once a chicken contracted barracks sickness an internee would catch it and take the bird to his barracks where it would later die. [17]

Estelle Ishigo stands near items discarded by internees as the camp was being closed (BSC).

Ota worked for the WRA until the livestock program was discontinued. During his employment at the camp, Ota met Masako Matsuda, an evacuee from Los Angeles. In 1944 Ota and Matsuda were married. When his employment with the WRA ended, Dr. Ota moved to nearby Lovell where he started a family and a thriving veterinary practice. [18]

When it was decided that the farm project would not continue into the summer of 1945, all of the equipment and supplies, the tractors, plows and seed and fertilizer were declared surplus. All of the surplus items were auctioned off which enabled area farmers to purchase the seed and equipment at fire-sale prices. The land which had been farmed in the previous two years reverted to the Reclamation Service. The Reclamation Service in turn rented the land to farmers in the Powell and Cody area. Sealed bids were submitted with the land being leased to the highest bidder. [19]

Upon hearing that some residents at Heart Mountain were hoping to stay in the camp instead of leaving, the Wyoming Legislature went into action. Members of the state senate and house of representatives misinterpreted the wish of some internees to stay in camp as an intention by internees to settle in Wyoming. The legislators were in a panic and grasping at straws in an effort to find some way to discourage the Japanese from remaining in the state. The only thing legislators could come up with was a law which barred former Heart Mountain residents from purchasing Wyoming hunting and fishing licenses. The law stated

> that any person who has been or is hereafter brought, or caused to be brought, into the State of Wyoming by the War Relocation Authority, or other similar agency, or who is now or hereafter interned in a relocation center, concentration camp, prisoner of war camp, or any other similar governmental facility established in Wyoming, under any national emergency which has been or is hereafter proclaimed by the President of the United States, shall not be entitled to a hunting or fishing license or permit, . . . [20]

The bill was approved on February 15, 1945 and signed into law by Governor Lester Hunt. [21]

By June 1945, twenty-five percent of the internees still refused to make any plans to relocate. The population had dropped to approximately 6,800, but there remained a concerted effort by the residents to maintain the facilities indefinitely. The Community Council was doing everything in its power to persuade the administration to keep the schools open for the autumn term. At that time the target date for closing the camp was still set at January of 1946. Nevertheless, the administration had already decided that the schools would not be opened in the fall. Robertson and others believed that closing the schools would help force the residents out of the camp sooner. Robertson's excuse for giving no consideration to keeping the schools open was that those complaining about it were part of a small minority. [22]

A number of those residing in relocation centers said that the WRA was the only friend they had during the war. This was, in many instances, true. But when it came time for the camps to close, the WRA was more concerned with meeting closing date deadlines than with the future welfare of the internees. The decision to close the schools was only one example of this. Dillon Myer was approached with the fact that when it came time to close the camps he was in effect giving the internees $25 and throwing them out. There were those on the outside who believed that a little more money would have given the evacuees a better chance to start over. Myer said that the $25 for "those returning to their former homes and those taking up residence elsewhere–is entirely adequate for their needs." [23]

By July it was reported that during the first six months since the declaration of "X-DAY," 2,209 internees had left the center. Many more still had to be relocated, and time was running out. It was also in July when Dillon Myer announced that the date for closing Heart Mountain had been moved up to November 15, 1945.

Residents in the camp were still fighting the removal date and the $25 relocation allowance. One man who was asked why he had not yet relocated said he could not afford to. He explained that the evacuees gave up their livelihood and their means of support in an effort to do what the government was asking of them. He felt that doing so created some sort of obligation on the part of the government to help internees get back on their feet. The $25 that the government was paying was not only an insult, it was not a realistic sum with which to get back a family's land and belongings. [24]

With the date for the closing of the camp having been moved up, the administration hurried to have the evacuees finish making arrangements to leave the center. The process of relocation planning was to end by October 1. Any internees who had not made arrangements as far as a date of departure and destination by that date would have it done for them. In other words, if some residents were determined to remain in the camp, the administration would choose their date of departure and send them back to the area from which they were originally evacuated. Residents would have their belongings packed for them and would be physically put on the train if necessary, as was the case with Mrs. Serisawa. [25]

On July 28, the *Heart Mountain Sentinel* issued its final edition. From that point on, the closing of the camp moved along rather quickly. The stores in the center began to close, and the major item of concern for the residents was finding a house or apartment to move into back home. Guy Robertson said he believed the internees were making a genuine effort to get out of the camp, but were having problems finding any type of housing. Twenty-five Catholic families requested permission to send a representative to Los Angeles to ask the priest in their old neighborhood, Father Lavery, if he could help them arrange for some sort of temporary housing. The administration was also receiving complaints from some former internees who had already relocated to Los Angeles. The government had contracted with Lyons Van and Storage to deliver the evacuees' personal belongings to their residences in California. Lyons picked up the belongings and delivered them, but was charging the owners up to $50 in delivery fees. [26]

By September 1 there were still nearly 4,500 residents at Heart Mountain. Robertson worried that he was going to have to forcibly remove a number of them in order to meet the November 15 deadline. He felt that he was looking at a potential problem since the MP's were scheduled to leave camp on September 4. Robertson hoped that the surrender of Japan and the official ending of the war would increase the speed with which the residents left the camp, but it did not. [27]

Nevertheless, the camp closed ahead of schedule. The last train of evacuees left on Saturday night at 8:00 p.m., November 10, 1945. The administration had slowly closed down the facilities around the residents. Once it was evident that the camp would close, the evacuees left whether they had a home to return to or not. Some of those with nowhere to go ended up in trailer parks in very small units which the WRA had set up as a form of temporary housing. The trailers were rented for $15 per month. Shortly after the trailer camp was established, the WRA shut off the electricity in an effort once again to force the evacuees to move on. After several fires resulting from the use of kerosene lamps, the fire department ordered the electricity turned back on. When the WRA walked away from any responsibility for the camp in May of 1946, there were still 1,800 people in the Los

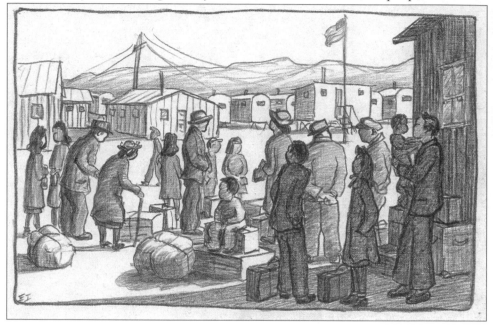

WRA trailer camp at Burbank, California, November 13, 1945. Drawing by Estelle Ishigo (BSC).

Angeles area alone with no place to go. [28]

In his final report, Robertson said that even though the evacuees were gone, he and his staff would probably remain at Heart Mountain until the first of the year. The *Powell Tribune* reported that the Japanese were gone. An editorial said the evacuees had been taken back where they came from, and described Heart Mountain as a ghost town. The editorial concluded by saying, "The Japanese were well treated here and the whole circumstance of their relocation passes off with few disturbing memories." [29]

Epilogue

As Japanese Americans returned to the West Coast, they quickly found that the attitudes of some people had changed little. Personal property–businesses, farms and homes not sold prior to evacuation–were found ransacked or abused and neglected by lessees. Some businesses refused to buy produce from Japanese farmers and local politicians sometimes did everything in their power to halt the issuing of business licenses to those returning from the camps. In California, there were still attempts by the state government to dispossess former internees of the land they owned.

Personal property sold in evacuation sales for $10 often cost $150 to $200 to replace. The long-term economic loss to those evacuated and interned was estimated by the Federal Reserve Bank at $400,000,000. On July 2, 1948, President Harry Truman signed the Japanese Evacuation Claims Act to compensate former internees for property losses resulting from the evacuation. In time, the government paid $38,000,000 on evacuation claims. This amount was less than ten cents on every dollar lost. When adjusted for inflation, the payments actually amounted to a settlement of approximately five cents for every dollar lost.

In California, the state legislature encouraged the confiscation of land belonging to Nisei if that land was purchased illegally by an Issei and then placed in the name of a dependent child. In *The People vs. Oyama*, the Supreme Court ruled six to three that the land confiscations by the state of California were illegal. The court ruled that the confiscations were discriminatory and based solely on the fact that the Nisei's father was Japanese. Soon after the Oyama decision, the California Alien Land Law was removed from the statutes.

At the national level, the passage of the Walter-McCarran Immigration and Naturalization Act of 1952 repealed the Oriental Exclusion aspects of the 1924 Immigration Act. The Walter-McCarran Act also eliminated race as a consideration in determining an immigrant's eligibility for United States citizenship. In 1976, the year of the American Bicentennial, President Gerald Ford repealed Executive Order 9066. Several years later, in 1980, President Jimmy Carter and Congress created the Commission on the Wartime Relocation and Internment of Civilians. Three years later, the Redress Commission issued a report entitled *Personal Justice Denied*. That report stated that relocation could not be justified under the guise of military necessity. It stated further that relocation came about as a result of war hysteria, racial prejudice, and a failure on the part of political leadership. In 1990 the federal government issued a check for $20,000 each and a signed apology from President George Bush to all surviving former internees.

In Wyoming, following the war, the Heart Mountain Reclamation Project

139

was opened to homesteaders. The site on which the Heart Mountain Relocation Center was once located is now farm land. Until the late 1960's, barracks buildings which once housed internees could be seen on nearly every farm between the towns of Powell and Cody. Today, a memorial garden, the Heart Mountain Hospital chimney, and several camp buildings are all that remain of the site which was once Wyoming's third largest community. Former Heart Mountain internees and Wyoming historical groups work to preserve what remains of the camp site in an effort to remind us, and future generations, what results when hysteria and prejudice are allowed to prevail.

Estelle Ishigo with stray dogs that wandered into camp (BSC).

Introduction

1.Ronald Takaki, *Strangers from a Different Shore: A History of Asian Americans* (New York: Penguin Books, 1989), 31-32, 82. Roger Daniels, *Prisoners Without Trial: Japanese Americans in World War II* (New York: Hill & Wang, 1993), 6-7.

2.Takaki, *Strangers from a Different Shore, 84-91.*

3.Roger Daniels, *The Politics of Prejudice: The Anti-Japanese Movement in California and the Struggle for Japanese Exclusion* (Berkeley: University of California Press, 1977), 7. Daniels, *Prisoners Without Trial, 6-7.*

4.William L. Neumann, *America Encounters Japan: From Perry to MacArthur* (Baltimore: Johns Hopkins University Press, 1963), 43-45, 60-61. Gary Y. Okihiro, *Cane Fires: The Anti-Japanese Movement in Hawaii, 1865-1945* (Philadelphia: Temple University Press, 1991), 20. Yuji Ichioka, *The Issei: The World of the First Generation Japanese Immigrants, 1885-1924* (New York: Free Press, 1988), 3-4.

5.Ichioka, *The Issei,* 8-9, 28, 50-52.

6.Daniels, *The Politics of Prejudice,* 27-28.

7.Daniels, *Prisoners Without Trial,* 9-13. Daniels, *The Politics of Prejudice,* 31-33.

8.Daniels, *Prisoners Without Trial,* 12-13. Daniels, *The Politics of Prejudice,* 31-37.

9.Daniels, *The Politics of Prejudice,* 40-44.

10.Daniels, *The Politics of Prejudice,* 9-10. Ichioka, *The Issei,* 96-102. David J. O'Brien and Stephen S. Fujiita, *The Japanese American Experience* (Bloomington: Indiana University Press, 1991), 19-20.

11.Daniels, *Prisoners Without Trial,* 13-14.

12.Daniels, *The Politics of Prejudice,* 44-45. Daniels, *Prisoners Without Trial,* 14. O'Brien and Fugita, *The Japanese American Experience,* 24.

13.Daniels, *The Politics of Prejudice,* 89-91. Frank Van Nuys, "Sowing the Seeds of Internment: James D. Phelan's Anti-Japanese Crusade, 1919-1920," in *Remembering Heart Mountain: Essays on Japanese American Internment in Wyoming,* ed. Mike Mackey (Powell WY: Western History Publications, 1998), 6-7.

14.Daniels, *The Politics of Prejudice,* 90-91. O'Brien and Fujita, *The Japanese American Experience,* 24-25.

15.Daniels, *Prisoners Without Trial,* 15. For a detailed look at the effects of the 1924

Immigration Act on Japanese living in the United States at that time see, Ichioka, The Issei, 244-54.

16.Daniels, *Prisoners Without Trial*, 16-21. O'Brien and Fugita, *The Japanese American Experience*, 39-42.

Chapter 1

1.Francis Biddle, Justice Department News Release, December 8, 1941, Joseph C. O'Mahoney Collection, American Heritage Center, University of Wyoming.

2.Louis Fiset, *Imprisoned Apart: The World War II Correspondence of an Issei Couple* (Seattle: University of Washington Press, 1997), 30-31. Bill Hosokawa, *Out of the Frying Pan: Reflections of a Japanese American* (Niwot: University Press of Colorado, 1998), 42-43.

3.Justice Department, "Instructions to United States Attorneys," O'Mahoney Collection.

4.Hosokawa, *Out of the Frying Pan*, 31-32.

5.Hosokawa, *Nisei: The Quiet Americans* (New York: William Morrow and Company, 1969, reprinted, Niwot: University Press of Colorado, 1992), 236-37.

6.Justice Department News Release, December 13, 1941, O'Mahoney Collection. Hosokawa, *Nisei*, 253.

7."Short-Wave Foundling," *Newsweek*, January 19, 1942, 25.

8.Department of Justice News Release, December 28, 1941, O'Mahoney Collection.

9."California and the Japanese," *The New Republic*, March 2, 1942, 295-96. Hosokawa, *Out of the Frying Pan*, 28. John Tateishi, *And Justice for All* (New York: Random House, 1984, reprinted, Seattle: University of Washington Press, 1999), 60-61. Estelle Ishigo, *Lone Heart Mountain* (Santa Clara, CA: Communicart, 1972), 3-4. Ruth Hashimoto to author, October 23, 1992.

10.Department of Justice, *Ex Parte Kumezo Kawato*, Circular No. 3763, December 3, 1943, O'Mahoney Collection.

11.Daniels, *Prisoners Without Trial*, 26-27. Hosokawa, *Nisei*, 252-53.

12.Hosokawa, *Out of the Frying Pan*, 27-28.

13.Roger Daniels, "Incarcerating Japanese Americans: An Atrocity Revisited," in *Remembering Heart Mountain: Essays on Japanese American Internment in Wyoming*, ed. Mike Mackey, 20-21. Daniels, *Prisoners Without Trial*, 28-29.

14.Daniels, *Prisoners Without Trial*, 30-32.

15.Ibid., Daniels, "Incarcerating Japanese Americans," 22.

16.Daniels, *Prisoners Without Trial*, 38-41. Hosokawa, *Out of the Frying Pan*, 29. "The Shape of Things," *The Nation*, February 21, 1942, 206.

17.Robert E. Herzstein, *Henry R. Luce: A Political Portrait of the Man Who Created the American Century* (New York: Macmillan Publishing Company, 1994), 162-76, 217-33, 251. *Life*, March 2, 1942, 16-17.

18."Japanese Carry War to California Coast," *Life*, March 9, 1942, 19.

19."Japanese Roundup," *The Nation*, March 9, 1942, 27-28.

20.Carey McWilliams, "California and the Japanese," *The New Republic*, March 2, 1942, 296.

21.Louis Fischer, "West Coast Perspective," *The Nation*, March 7, 1942.

22.Richard Lee Strout, "The War and Civil Liberties," *The New Republic*, March 16, 1942, 356.

23.Daniels, *Prisoners Without Trial*, 40.

24."Seaboard Safeguard," *The Nation*, March 2, 1942, 29.

25.McWilliams, "California and the Japanese," 295.

26.Michi Weglyn, *Years of Infamy: The Untold Story of America's Concentration Camps* (New York: William Morrow and Company, Inc., 1976), 69. Daniels, *Prisoners Without Trial*, 43-47.

27.Daniels, *Prisoners Without Trial*, 44, 129-30.

28.Hosokawa, *Nisei*, 287.

29.Hosokawa, *Out of the Frying Pan*, 30.

Chapter 2

1.Nels Smith to all county sheriffs, December 12, 1941, Nels Smith Collection, American Heritage Center, University of Wyoming.

2.Frank Blackburn to Nels Smith, January 31, 1942, Smith Collection.

3.Nels Smith to Department of War and United States Attorney General, February 21, 1942, Smith Collection.

4.Ibid.

5.Ora Bever to Nels Smith, February 23, 1942, Smith Collection.

6.Walter Matson to Nels Smith, February 23, 1942, Smith Collection.

7.T. A. Larson, *Wyoming's War Years 1941-1945* (Palo Alto: Stanford University Press, 1954, reprinted, Cheyenne: Wyoming Historical Foundation, 1993), 305.

8.*Cody Enterprise*, February 25, 1942.

9.T. A. Larson, *History of Wyoming* (Lincoln: University of Nebraska Press, 1965, revised, 1978), 411-13. Mike Mackey, *Black Gold: Patterns in the Development of Wyoming's Oil Industry* (Powell WY: Western History Publications, 1997) 58, 98.

10.R. T. Baird, *Powell Tribune*, February 26, 1942.

11.Kenneth Kellar to Nels Smith, March 4, 1942, Smith Collection.

12.Ibid.

13.Ibid.

14.E. L. Bennett to Nels Smith, March 23, 1942, Smith Collection.

15.N. Smith to Nels Smith, August 8, 1942, Smith Collection.

16.Ibid.

17.Ibid.

18.Ralph T. Fisher to Nels Smith, March 11, 1942, Smith Collection.

19.Charles Inglehart, "Citizens Behind Barbed Wire," *The Nation*, June 6, 1942, 651. J. W. Decker to Nels Smith, June 12, 1942, Smith Collection.

20.A. B. Maycock to Nels Smith, March 11, 1942, Smith Collection.

21.W. J. Gorst to Nels Smith, March 17, 1942, Smith Collection.

22.J. N. Rickinpaugh to Nels Smith, March 18, 1942, Smith Collection.

23.Foster W. Jones to Nels Smith, April 3, 1942 and William E. Mau to Nels Smith, April 5, 1942, Smith Collection.

24.C. S. Porter to Nels Smith, March 6, 1942, Smith Collection.

25.Milton Eisenhower to Nels Smith, March 30, 1942, Smith Collection. Weglyn, *Years of Infamy*, 84.

26."Japanese Roundup," *The Nation*, 28. Sandra C. Taylor, *Jewel of the Desert: Japanese*

American Internment at Topaz (Berkeley: University of California Press, 1993), 100, 107.

27.Daniels, *Prisoners Without Trial*, 57.

28."Japanese Roundup," 28. Hosokawa, *Nisei*, 225-26.

29.W. C. Miller to Nels Smith, March 17, 1942, Smith Collection.

30.Nels Smith to W. C. Miller, March 18, 1942, Smith Collection.

31.Ibid.

32.Chester Ingle to Nels Smith, April 20, 1942, Smith Collection.

33.Nels Smith to Henry Stimson, July 8 1942, Smith Collection.

34.Henry Stimson to Nels Smith, July 21 1942, Smith Collection.

Chapter 3

1.Daniels, *Prisoners Without Trial*, 51-53.

2.*Personal Justice Denied: Report of the Commission on Wartime Relocation and Internment of Civilians* (Washington: Government Printing Office, 1982), Daniels, *Prisoners Without Trial*, 54.

3.Ibid., 109-10.

4.Daniels, *Prisoners Without Trial*, 53-55.

5.Weglyn, *Years of Infamy*, 76-77.

6.For a more detailed look at The Children's Village see, Lisa Nobe, "The Children's Village at Manzanar: The World War II Eviction and Detention of Japanese American Orphans," *Journal of the West*, April 1999, 65-71.

7.Frank B. Duveneck, "Evacuating American Citizens," *The Nation*, May 9, 1942, 556.

8.Ibid.

9.John Modell, ed., *The Kikuchi Diary: Chronicle of an American Concentration Camp* (Chicago: University of Illinois Press, 1993), 51-53.

10.Daniels, *Prisoners Without Trial*, 55. Ted Nakashima, "Concentration Camp: U. S. Style," *The New Republic*, June 15, 1942, 822-23.

11.Daniels, *Prisoners Without Trial*, 55. John Kitasako, "Heart Mountain Glimpses," *Powell Tribune*, April 1, 1943.

12.Modell, *The Kikuchi Diary*, 51.

13.Ben Okura interview with Bacon Sakatani, West Covina, California, March 9, 1993.

14.Ibid.

15.Mike Hatchimonji to author, October 27, 1992. Ike Hatchimonji to author, October 15, 1992.

16.Ibid.

17.Frank Hayami to author, October 16, 1992.

18.Jean Ushijima to author, November 10, 1992.

19.Yas Ikeda to author, October 26, 1992.

20.Joyce Mori to author, December 22, 1992.

21.Yosh Sogioka to author, December 5, 1992.

22.Ibid.

23.Tatsu Hori to author, March 1, 1993. Tatsu Hori interview with Sam Conley, San Jose State University, date unknown.

24.Weglyn, *Years of Infamy*, 77.

25.Rose Yamashiro to author, September 19, 1992.

26.Art Tsuneishi to author, November 13, 1992. Toyoo Nitake to author, November 28, 1992. Jack Oda to author, May 6, 1993.

27.Toshiko Ito to author, October 22, 1992.

28.Ibid.

29.Jack Tono to author, February 11, 1993.

30.Ruth Hashimoto to author, October 23, 1992.

31.Mori Shimada to author, February 5, 1993. Emi Kuromiya to author, November 11, 1992.

32.Dyaney Ota to Nels Smith, August 1, 1942, Smith Collection.

33.Ibid.

Chapter 4

1.Joseph O'Mahoney to Ray Bower, April 9, 1942, O'Mahoney Collection.

2.A. B. Chapman to Joseph O'Mahoney, April 11, 1942 and L. E. Laird to O'Mahoney, April 28, 1942, O'Mahoney Collection.

3.A. B. Chapman to Joseph O'Mahoney, April 11, 1942, O'Mahoney Collection.

4.B. M. Bryan to Nels Smith, May 2, 1942, Smith Collection. Milton Eisenhower to Joseph O'Mahoney, May 4, 1942, O'Mahoney Collection.

5.Joseph O'Mahoney to A. B. Chapman, June 3, 1942; Chapman to O'Mahoney, May 27, 1942 and John J. McCloy to O'Mahoney, July 25, 1942, O'Mahoney Collection.

6.Harry Attebery to Joseph O'Mahoney, May 13, 1942, O'Mahoney Collection.

7.Paul Greever to Joseph C. O'Mahoney, May 11, 1942; Paul Stock to Joseph O'Mahoney, May 12, 1942; Harry Attebery to Joseph O'Mahoney, May 13, 1942; Don Jamison to Joseph O'Mahoney, May 26, 1942; Jack Richard to Joseph O'Mahoney, May 23, 1942, O'Mahoney Collection.

8.*Powell Tribune*, June 4, 1942.

9.Ibid.

10.*Powell Tribune*, June 11, and June 18, 1942. *Cody Enterprise*, June 3, 1942.

11.*Powell Tribune*, July 9, 1942.

12.Ibid.

13.George Reesy to Joseph O'Mahoney, June 20, 1942, O'Mahoney Collection.

14.Paul Greever to Joseph O'Mahoney, June 29, 1942 and J. A. Morrow to Joseph O'Mahoney, June 30, 1942, O'Mahoney Collection.

15.Richard Jones to Joseph O'Mahoney, July 2, 1942; Paul Greever to Joseph O'Mahoney, August 11, 1942; Oliver Steadman to Joseph O'Mahoney, August 12, 1942, O'Mahoney Collection.

16.*Powell Tribune*, July 30, 1942.

17.*Powell Tribune*, August 20, 1942 and October 1, 1942.

Notes

18.*Powell Tribune*, January 18, 1943.

19.*Powell Tribune*, September 24, 1942.

20.*Heart Mountain Sentinel*, October 31, 1942 and November 21, 1942. *Powell Tribune*, January 7, 1943. Al Fryer to Lester Hunt, June 21, 1944, Lester Hunt Collection, American Heritage Center, University of Wyoming. *Powell Tribune*, September 2, 1944.

21.Louis Fiset, "Thinning, Topping, and Loading: Japanese Americans and Beet Sugar in World War II," *Pacific Northwest Quarterly* 90 (Summer 1999): 123-39.

22.*Powell Tribune*, August 13 and September 3, 1942.

23.Nels Smith to Joseph O'Mahoney, September 17, 1942, O'Mahoney Collection.

24.Ibid.

25.Ibid.

26.G. W. Hardy to Joseph O'Mahoney, September 15, 1942; John Fowler to Joseph O'Mahoney, September 15, 1942; Phil Schuman to O'Mahoney, September 15, 1942; Paul Pabst to Joseph O'Mahoney, September 15, 1942; Harry Kaiser to O'Mahoney, September 15, 1942, O'Mahoney Collection.

27.Nels Smith to Joseph O'Mahoney, September 17, 1942, O'Mahoney Collection.

28.Fiset, "Thinning, Topping, and Loading," 134.

29.P. B. Smith to Joseph O'Mahoney, September 21 1942, O'Mahoney Collection. *Cody Enterprise*, September 2, 1942.

30.*Powell Tribune*, September 24, and October 8, 1942. John McElroy to Joseph O'Mahoney, September 28, 1942, O'Mahoney Collection.

31.Alex Kaufmann to Joseph O'Mahoney, September 25, 1942, O'Mahoney Collection.

32.W. E. Pearson to Joseph O'Mahoney, October 13, 1942, O'Mahoney Collection.

33.*Heart Mountain Sentinel*, October 24, 1942, 8.

34.Joseph Smart to Joseph O'Mahoney, October 14, 1942 and Dillon Myer to Joseph O'Mahoney, October 21, 1942, O'Mahoney Collection. Fiset, "Thinning, Topping, and Loading," 133.

35.*Powell Tribune*, December 24, 1942.

Chapter 5

1.*Powell Tribune*, August 13, 1942.

2.Ibid., *Powell Tribune*, July 30, 1942.

3.John Nelson diary, August 11, 1942, TS, Nelson Collection, American Heritage Center, University of Wyoming. Ben Okura interview.

4.Bea Araki to author, December 2, 1992. John Nelson diary, August 28, 1942. Hosokawa, *Out of the Frying Pan*, 41-42.

5.Bea Araki to author, December 2, 1992. Jack Oda to author, May 6, 1993. Toshiko Ito to author, October 22, 1992. Frank Hayami to author, October 16, 1992. Kara Kondo to author, December 10, 1992.

6.Yosh Sogioka to author, December 5, 1992. Ruth Hashimoto to author, October 23, 1992. Rose Yamashiro to author, September 19, 1992.

7.Ada Endo to author, November 30, 1992. John Nelson diary, August 30, 1942.

8.*Powell Tribune*, September 10, 1942. WRA history and description of the Heart Mountain Relocation Center, Japanese American Evacuation and Resettlement Papers, hereafter cited as (JAERP), M1.00, Bancroft Library, University of California, Berkeley.

9.Toshiko Ito to author, October 22, 1992.

10.Frank Hayami to author, October 16, 1992. Jean Ushijima to author, November 10, 1992.

11.Douglas W. Nelson, "Heart Mountain: The History of an American Concentration Camp," (master's thesis, University of Wyoming, 1970), 30.

12.WRA report on living conditions, October 1942, JAERP, M1.00. Toyoo Nitake to author, November 28, 1992.

13.Yas Ikeda to author, October 26, 1992. Yosh Sogioka to author, December 5, 1992. Mike Hatchimonji to author, October 15, 1992.

14.Frank Cross report, JAERP, M1.00.

15.Nelson, "Heart Mountain," 30.

16.Ike Hatchimonji to author, October 27, 1992.

17.Kazuko Tokeshi to author, October 30, 1992. John Nelson diary, August 30, September 3, and 11, 1942.

18. Mess halls report, September 21, 1942, JAERP, M1.00. Nelson, "Heart Mountain," 30-31.

19. Ibid.

20. *Heart Mountain Sentinel*, October 24, 1942, 4. Harold Stanley Jacoby, *Tule Lake: From Relocation to Segregation* (Grass Valley, CA: Comstock Bonanza Press, 1996), 19.

21. Ibid.

22. Frank Hayami to author, October 16, 1992.

23. John Nelson diary, August 28, 1942. Community Organization reports, JAERP, M1.00.

24. Community Organization report, JAERP, M1.00.

25. Ibid.

26. Ibid. Bill Hosokawa to author, September 22, 1992. Nelson, "Heart Mountain," 37.

27. Ibid., 38.

28. Hosokawa, *Out of the Frying Pan*, 50-51.

29. Ibid., 14-16, 50-51.

30. *Heart Mountain Sentinel*, October 24, 1942. Bill Hosokawa to author, September 22, 1992. Camp reports, JAERP, M1.00.

31. Bill Hosokawa to author, September 22, 1992. Naomi Sasano to author, January 18, 1993. Hosokawa, *Out of the Frying Pan*, 51.

32. *Heart Mountain Sentinel*, October 16, 1943.

Chapter 6

1. *Powell Tribune*, September 24, 1942. *Heart Mountain Sentinel*, October 28, 1943. Velma Kessel, "Remembering the Heart Mountain Hospital," in *Remembering Heart Mountain*, 191-92.

2. Yosh Sogioka to author, December 5, 1992.

3. Emi Kuromiya to author, November 11, 1942. Ada Endo to author, November 30, 1992.

4. Ibid.

5. Arthur L. Kerr, final report, Fire Protection Section, September 28, 1945, JAERP M2.90.

Notes

6.Ibid. Bill Hosokawa to author, September 30, 1993.

7.John Kitasako, "Heart Mountain Glimpses," *Powell Tribune*, February 5, 1943.

8.Louis Fiset, "The Heart Mountain Hospital Strike of June 24, 1943," in *Remembering Heart Mountain*, 101.

9.Kessel, "Heart Mountain Hospital," 187-88. Fiset, "Hospital Strike," 102.

10.John Kitasako, "Heart Mountain Glimpses," *Powell Tribune*, April 1, 1943. Toshiko Ito to author, October 22, 1992. Fiset, "Hospital Strike," 101.

11.John Kitasako, "Heart Mountain Glimpses," *Powell Tribune*, April 1, 1943. Fiset, "Hospital Strike," 105, 107. Kessel, "Heart Mountain Hospital," 187.

12.Emi Kuromiya to author, November 11, 1942. Ada Endo to author, November 30, 1992. Mori Shimada to author, February 5, 1993. Naomi Sassano to author, January 18, 1993.

13.Kessel, "Heart Mountain Hospital," 189.

14.John Kitasako, "Heart Mountain Glimpses," *Powell Tribune*, April 1, 1943. Kessel, "Heart Mountain Hospital," 190.

15.Mike Hatchimonji to author, October 15, 1992. Toshiko Ito to author, October 22, 1992.

16.Yas Ikeda to author, October 26, 1992.

17.Mike Hatchimonji to author, October 15, 1992. Emi Kuromiya to author, November 11, 1992. Eugene Sasai to author, March 7, 1993.

18.John Kitasako, "Heart Mountain Glimpses," *Powell Tribune*, March 4, 1943.

19.Byron Ver Ploeg, Final Report of the Project Attorney, December 6, 1945, JAERP M1.30.

20.*Powell Tribune*, November 22, 1945, September 10, 1942 and September 17, 1942.

21.*Powell Tribune*, November 12, 1942. *Heart Mountain Sentinel*, November 14, 1942.

22.Raymond Uno to author, May 2, 1993. Amy Uno Ishi, oral history interview by Betty E. Mitson and Kristin Mitchell, July 9 and 20, 1973, California State University, Fullerton, Oral History Program, Japanese American Project, Wyoming State Archives, Cheyenne, Wyoming. *Heart Mountain Sentinel*, January 9, 1943.

23.John Nelson diary, September 9, 1942. *Heart Mountain Sentinel*, November 14, 1942.

24.*Heart Mountain Sentinel*, January 9, 1943.

25.Ibid., February 13, 1943.

26.Ibid. *Powell Tribune*, January 28, 1943. Raymond Uno to author, May 2, 1993.

27.Mike Hatchimonji to author, October 15, 1992.

28.Ibid. Raymond Uno to author, May 2, 1993. Eugene Sasai to author, March 7, 1993. Ike Hatchimonji to author, October 27, 1993. Rose Yamashiro to author, September 19, 1992.

29.Kara Kondo, "Greatest Gift," unpublished paper in author's possession, December 1978.

30.Ibid. Ada Endo to author, November 30, 1992.

Chapter 7

1.J. K. Corbett, Final Report on Education at Heart Mountain, JAERP M1.74. Mamoru Inouye, "Heart Mountain High School, 1942-1945," *Journal of the West*, April 1999, 57. For a detailed review of the Heart Mountain High School see, Mamoru Inouye, "Heart Mountain High School, 1942-1945, in *Remembering Heart Mountain*.

2.Corbett, Final Report on Education. *Powell Tribune*, August 13, 1942. Kaoru Inouye to author, November 16, 1992. Inouye, "Heart Mountain High School," 57.

3.Corbett, Final Report on Education. Inouye, "Heart Mountain High School," 57. Thomas James, *Exile Within: The Schooling of Japanese Americans 1942-1945*. (Cambridge: Harvard University Press, 1987), 43.

4.Ibid.

5.Ibid. Yas Ikeda to author, October 26, 1992. "Heart Mountain High School," 58. Paul L. Christensen, "An Evaluation of Certain Phases of Heart Mountain Elementary Schools" (master's thesis, University of Wyoming, 1943), 85-86.

6.Ibid. Yas Ikeda to author, October 26, 1992.

7.Corbett, Final Report on Education. Christensen, "Heart Mountain Elementary School," 62, 70.

8.Corbett, Final Report on Education. *Heart Mountain Sentinel*, October 24, 1942, 8.

9.Inouye, "Heart Mountain High School," 59.

10.Corbett, Final Report on Education. *Billings Gazette*, June 22, 1986. Inouye, "Heart Mountain High School," 59-60.

11.Corbett, Final Report on Education.

12.Ibid. Inouye, "Heart Mountain High School," 62.

13.John Kitasako, "Heart Mountain Glimpses," *Powell Tribune*, July 15, September 30 and October 14, 1943.

14.Evacuee-Administration Relations Report, September 1, 1943, JAERP M1.00. Clarissa Corbett files, interview, American Heritage Center, University of Wyoming. Inouye, "Heart Mountain High School," 63.

15.Yas Ikeda to author, October 29, 1992. Jean Ushijima to author, November 10, 1992. Ike Hatchimonji to author, October 27, 1992. Mike Hatchimonji to author, October 15, 1992.

16.Raymond Uno to author, May 2, 1993. Christensen, "Heart Mountain Elementary Schools," 75. James, *Exile Within*, 140-41.

17.Bea Araki to author, December 2, 1992. Clarissa Corbett interview, Corbett file.

18.Kaoru Inouye to author, November 19, 1992.

19.Ibid.

20.Corbett, Final Report on Education.

21.Christensen, "Heart Mountain Elementary School," 23-24.

22.James, *Exile Within*, 72-73.

23.Ibid., 38. Inouye, "Heart Mountain High School," 58.

24.James, *Exile Within*, 72-73.

25.Ibid., 113, 134-35.

26.Ibid., 141, 144.

Chapter 8

1.T. J. O'Mara, Community Activities Section Final Report, JAERP M2. 10.

2.Ibid.

3.Ibid. *Heart Mountain Sentinel*, October 24, 1942.

4.Ibid. *Powell Tribune*, September 24, 1942. Mary Oyama, "Heart Mountain Breezes," *Tribune*, December 10, 1942.

Notes

5.*Powell Tribune*, October 1, 1942. Mike Hatchimonji to author, October 15, 1992. Bea Araki to author, December 2, 1992.

6.O'Mara, Community Activities Report. May Oyama, "Heart Mountain Breezes, *Powell Tribune*, November 5, 1942. *Powell Triune*, October 1, 1942.

7.O'Mara, Community Activities Report.

8.Ibid. Mori Shimada to author, February 5, 1993.

9.O'Mara, Community Activities Report.

10.Ibid. Thomas Kinaga to author, December 18, 1992. Bea Araki to author, December 2, 1992. Jean Ushijima to author, November 10, 1992. Arthur Tsuneishi to author, November 13, 1992.

11.Office of Project Director Report, JAERP M1.00. Asael T. Hansen, "My Two Years at Heart Mountain: The Difficult Role of an Applied Anthropologist," in *Japanese Americans: From Relocation to Redress*, eds. Roger Daniels, Sandra C. Taylor and Harry H. L. Kitano (Salt Lake: University of Utah Press, 1986, revised, Seattle: University of Washington Press, 1991), 34.

12.Raymond Uno to author, May 2, 1993. *Heart Mountain Sentinel*, October 24, 1942.

13.Toyoo Nitake to author, November 28, 1992. Mike Hatchimonji to author, October 15, 1992. Peter K. Simpson, "Recollections of Heart Mountain," in *Remembering Heart Mountain*, 183-84.

14.Toyoo Nitake to author, November 28, 1992. Mike Hatchimonji to author, October 15, 1992.

15.Yas Ikeda to author, October 26, 1992. Jean Ushijima to author, November 10, 1992. John Kitasako, "Heart Mountain Glimpses," *Powell Tribune*, May 6, May 13, and August 19, 1943.

16.O'Mara, Community Activities Report.

17.Ibid.

18.Ibid. Arthur Tsuneishi to author, November 13, 1992. Rose Yamashiro to author, September 19, 1992.

19.Jean Ushijima to author, November 10, 1992. O'Mara, Community Activities Report.

20.Naomi Sasano to author, January 18, 1993. Raymond Uno to author, May 2, 1993. Frank Hayami to author, October 16, 1992. John Kitasako, "Heart Mountain Glimpses," *Powell Tribune*, April 22, 1943.

21.John Kitasako, "Heart Mountain Glimpses," *Powell Tribune*, March 4, 1943.

22.Naomi Sasano to author, November 9, 1992. Frank Hayami to author, October 16, 1992. O'Mara, Community Activities Report.

23.Eugene Sasai to author, March 7, 1993. Ada Endo to author, November 30, 1992.

24.John Kitasako, "Heart Mountain Glimpses," *Powell Tribune*, April 15, 1943.

Chapter 9

1.W. Joe Carroll, Relocation Division Final Report, JAERP M1.60.

2.Ibid.

3.Ibid.

4.Ibid.

5.Ibid.

6.O'Brien and Fugita, *The Japanese American Experience*, 91. Jere Takahashi, *Nisei/Sansei: Shifting Japanese American Identities and Politics* (Philadelphia: Temple University Press, 1997), 102.

7.Hosokawa, *Out of the Frying Pan*, 57.

8.Ibid., 58-60.

9.Ruth Hashimoto to author, October 23, 1992.

10.Ibid.

11.Ibid.

12.Ibid.

13.Ibid.

14.Frank Hayami to author, October 16, 1992.

15.Mary Oyama, "Heart Mountain Breezes," *Powell Tribune*, January 28, 1943. *Heart Mountain Sentinel*, October 16, 1943.

16.Arthur Tsuneishi to author, November 13, 1992. Rose Yamashiro to author, September 19, 1992.

17. Ibid. Toshiko Ito to author, October 22, 1992.

18. Eugene Sasai to author, March 7, 1993.

19. Miyoko Eshita to author, May 2, 1993.

20. Ibid. *Powell Tribune*, November 12, 1942.

21. *Heart Mountain Sentinel*, August 28, 1943.

22. Jacoby, *Tule Lake*, 83.

23. Hosokawa, *Nisei*, 263-65.

24. Ibid.

25. Frank Hayami to author, October 16, 1992.

26. Jacoby, *Tule Lake*, 83. *Heart Mountain Sentinel*, September 18, August 21 and August 28, 1943.

27. Joyce Mori to author, December 22, 1992.

28. Ibid.

Chapter 10

1. *Cody Enterprise*, September 9, 1942.

2. *Powell Tribune*, September 10, 1942. John Nelson diary, September 9, 1942.

3. *Powell Tribune*, December 3, 1942.

4. Ibid.

5. Gordon A. Nicholson to J. Edgar Hoover, December 1, 1942, Japanese Relocation Files (JRF), FBI Records, National Archives, Washington D.C.

6. Ibid.

7. Ibid.

8. Ibid.

9. Ibid. J. Edgar Hoover to Edward Ennis, December 14, 1942, JRF, FBI records.

10. John Nelson diary, December 20, 1942.

11.Ibid.

12.*Powell Tribune*, November 5, 1942.

13.Ibid.

14.Nelson, "Heart Mountain," 46.

15.*Powell Tribune*, December 17, 1942.

16.Roberts, "Temporarily Side-Tracked by Emotionalism," in *Remembering Heart Mountain*, 45.

17.R. T. Baird, editorial, *Powell Tribune*, September 24, 1942. Mary Oyama, "Heart Mountain Breezes," *Powell Tribune*, December 17 and December 24, 1942.

18.John Nelson diary, January 17, 1943.

19.*Session Laws of Wyoming*, 1943, Chapter 27, Wyoming State Archives, Cheyenne, Wyoming.

20.*Powell Tribune*, January 21 and February 11, 1943.

21.Gordon Nicholson to J. Edgar Hoover, February 6, 1943, JRF, FBI records.

22.Ibid.

23.Guy Robertson to Lester Hunt, April 23, 1943, Lester Hunt Collection, American Heritage Center, University of Wyoming.

24.Ibid., Nelson, "Heart Mountain," 65.

25.*Powell Tribune*, May 6, 1943. Bill Hosokawa to author, September 22, 1992.

26.Ibid. John Nelson diary, September 7, 1942. *Cody Enterprise*, May 5, 1943.

27.John Nelson diary, May 7, 1943.

28.Ibid. *The Wyoming Eagle*, May 7, 1943.

29.*Heart Mountain Sentinel*, June 12, 1943.

30.*Cody Enterprise*, July 21, 1943.

31.*Heart Mountain Sentinel*, February 26, 1944.

32.*Powell Tribune*, May 27, 1943.

33.John Kitasako, "Heart Mountain Glimpses," *Powell Tribune*, June 24, 1943.

34.*Cody Enterprise*, September 15, 1943. *Heart Mountain Sentinel*, February 26, 1944.

35.*Heart Mountain Sentinel*, May 1, 1943.

36.Nelson, "Heart Mountain," 60, 75-76. Roberts, "Temporarily Side-Tracked by Emotionalism," 41-42, 44-45.

37.William Stone to Lester Hunt, April 24, 1943, Hunt Collection.

38.Lester Hunt to William Stone, April 26, 1943, Hunt Collection.

39.Ibid.

40.Harold Waechter to Lester Hunt, May 8, 1943, Hunt Collection.

41.Resolution adopted by VFW Post 1481, Ogden, Utah, September 1, 1943, Hunt Collection.

42.Ibid.

43.F. H. Dennison to Lester Hunt, November 30, 1943, Hunt Collection.

44.Ibid.

Chapter 11

1.Daniels, *Prisoners Without Trial*, 34-35.

2.Hosokawa, *Nisei*, 392, 397.

3.*Heart Mountain Sentinel*, January 9, 1943.

4.*Heart Mountain Sentinel*, February 20, 1943.

5.Ibid.

6.Ibid.

7.Ibid.

8.*Heart Mountain Sentinel*, February 27, 1943. Daniels, *Prisoners Without Trial*, 48.

9.Guy Robertson to the people of Heart Mountain, March 5, 1943, JAERP M2.40.

Notes

10.Ibid.

11.Ibid.

12.Guy Robertson to Dillon Myer, March 6, 1943, JAERP M2.40.

13.Report on Registration at Heart Mountain, March 9, 1943, JAERP M2.40.

14.Ibid. Frank Hayami to author, October 16, 1992. Toyoo Nitake to author, December 3, 1992.

15.Report on Registration at Heart Mountain.

16.Ibid.

17.*Heart Mountain Sentinel*, October 23, 1943. *Without Due Process*, directed and produced by Gerald and Misha Griffith, film documentary, KIXE televison, 1990.

18.*Heart Mountain Sentinel*, January 29 and February 5, 1944. Sam Fujishin, telephone interview with author, August 12, 1993. Sam Fujishin, "Nisei Soldiers: Their Contribution to Post World War II Japanese American Rights," in *Remembering Heart Mountain*, 143.

19.Ibid.

20.Jack Oda to author, May 6, 1993.

21.Ibid.

22.Frank Hayami to author, October 16, 1992.

23.Kaoru Inouye to author, November 16, 1992. Jack Oda to author, May 6, 1993. Hosokawa, *Nisei*, 398.

24.*Heart Mountain Sentinel*, February 26 and November 2, 1944.

25.*Heart Mountain Sentinel*, March 10, 1945. Franz Steidl, *Lost Battalions: Going For Broke in the Vosges, Autumn 1944* (Navato, CA: Persidio Press, 1997), 166.

26.Steidl, *Lost Battalions*, 191.

27.Steidl, *Lost Battalions*, 170-71.

28.Clarence Matsumura to author, February 4, 1993. Elaine Ruth Fletcher, "Dachau survivors reunited with their liberators," *San Francisco Examiner*, May 5, 1992. Larry Derfner, "Japanese-American liberators of Dachau meet survivors," *The Northern California Jewish Bulletin*, May 8, 1992.

29.Clarence Matsumura to author, February 4, 1993.

30.Solly Ganor, *Light One Candle: A Survivor's Tale from Lithuania to Jerusalem* (New York: Kodansha America, Inc., 1995), 335-43.

31.Ibid., 346-47.

32.Ibid.

33.*Powell Tribune*, November 22, 1945.

34.John Meyer, *Look Backs* (Long Prairie, MN: Neuman Press, 1984), 226.

Chapter 12

1."Fair Play Committee: We Should Know," JRF, FBI records, file 14-52.

2.Frank T. Inouye, "Immediate Origins of the Heart Mountain Draft Resistance Movement," in *Remembering Heart Mountain*, 121-26.

3.Ibid., 126-28.

4.Ibid. Guy Robertson, weekly report to Dillon Myer, February 12, 1944, JAERP M2.37.

5.Ibid. McMillen, FBI report 14-52. Guy Robertson, weekly report to Dillon Myer, February 19, 1944, JAERP M2.37.

6.Guy Robertson, weekly report to Dillon Myer, February 26, 1944, JAERP M2.37.

7.Fair Play Committee (FPC), petition to President Roosevelt, April 25, 1944, FBI records, file 14-52.

8.A. T. Anderson (Community Analyst), memorandum to M. O. Anderson (Assistant Project Director), March 10, 1944; Douglas Todd, weekly report to Dillon Myer, March 11, 1944, JAERP M2.37.

9.Guy Robertson, weekly report to Dillon Myer, March 18, 1944 and Douglas Todd, weekly report to Dillon Myer, March 27, 1944, JAERP M2.37.

10.Guy Robertson, weekly report to Dillon Myer, April 3, 1944, JAERP M2.37.

11.Ibid. Guy Robertson, weekly report to Dillon Myer, April 1, 1944, M2.37.

12.Hearing Board for Leave Clearance, Paul Nakadate, Ben Wakaye and Frank Emi, April 3 and 4, 1944, FBI records, file 14-52.

13.Guy Robertson to Dillon Myer, April 8, 1944, JAERP M2.37.

Notes

14.Arthur Hansen, "Sergeant Ben Kuroki's Perilous "Home Mission": Contested Loyalty and Patriotism in the Japanese American Detention Centers," in *Remembering Heart Mountain*, 153-57.

15.*Heart Mountain Sentinel*, April 15, 1944. Guy Robertson, weekly report to Dillon Myer, April 10, April 17 and May 13, 1944. Guy Robertson, Memorandum to Dillon Myer, April 15 and April 22, 1944, JAERP M2.37.

16.*The Wyoming Eagle*, May 11 and June 10, 1944. *United State vs. Fujii*, Criminal Case No. 4928, U. S. District Courts of the United States, Record Group 21, National Archives-Rocky Mountain Region, Denver, Colorado.

17.Jack Tono, notes from lecture given at Northeastern University, 1986, notes in author's possession.

18.Ibid. Jack Tono, lecture at University of Wyoming, October 19, 1993. Mits Koshiyama to author, August 25, 1993. *The Wyoming Eagle*, June 13, 1944.

19.Ibid.

20.William Minoru Hohri, *Repairing America: An Account of the Movement for Japanese-American Redress* (Pullman: Washington State University Press, 1988), 173-74. *The Wyoming Eagle*, June 15 and 16, 1944.

21.T. Blake Kennedy, Judge's Memorandum, June 26, 1944, *U. S. vs. Fujii*.

22.Ibid. *The Wyoming Eagle*, June 27, 1944.

23.Tateishi, *And Justice for All*, 174.

24.Tono notes, Northeastern University, 1986. Dillon Myer to Edward Ennis, May 15, 1944 and Edward Ennis to James Bennet, June 1, 1944, Japanese Relocation, Justice Department Files, National Archives, Washington D. C.

25.Arthur Hansen, "The 1944 Nisei Draft at Heart Mountain, Wyoming: Its Relationship to the Historical Representation of the World War II Japanese American Evacuation," *Magazine of History*, Summer 1996, 51.

26.Ibid. *United States vs. Kuwabara*, Criminal Case No. 8966-G, U. S. District Court for the District of Northern California, Records of District Courts of the United States, Record Group 21, National Archives-Rocky Mountain Region, Denver, Colorado. Inouye, "Draft Resistance Movement," 129-30.

27.Ibid. *Nichi Bei*, December 25, 1947.

28.Guy Robertson, weekly report to Dillon Myer, July 22, 1944, JAERP M2.37. *U. S. vs. Okamoto*, Criminal Case No. 4930, U. S. District Court for the District of Wyoming, Records of District Courts of the United States, Record Group 21, National Archives-Rocky Mountain Region, Denver, Colorado.

29.Ibid. Mits Koshiyama to author, January 8, 1993. *Heart Mountain Sentinel*, November 4, 1944. Hansen, "Home Mission," 158.

30.Inouye, "Draft Resistance Movement," 131.

31.Mits Koshiyama to author, January 8, 1993.

32.Ibid.

33.Jack Tono to author, February 11, 1993. Mits Koshiyama to author, January 8, 1993.

34.Ibid. Mits Koshiyama to author, August 25, 1993.

35.Hosokawa, *Nisei*, 423.

36.Ibid.

Chapter 13

1.John Nelson diary, December 20, 1942.

2.Minutes of joint council meeting of members from Powell and Cody Town Councils, April 24, 1943, Municipal Records, Cody City Hall, Cody Wyoming.

3.Ibid.

4.Minutes of Powell Town Council meeting, May 3, 1943, city records, Powell City Hall, Powell, Wyoming. Minutes of Cody Town Council meeting, May 3, 1943.

5.*Heart Mountain Sentinel*, May 8, 1943.

6.*Powell Tribune*, May 20, 1943.

7.Ibid. *Heart Mountain Sentinel*, May 29, 1943.

8.Minutes of Powell Town Council meeting, July 15, 1943.

9.Ibid.

10.*Powell Tribune*, August 12 and September 2, 1943.

Notes

11.*Heart Mountain Sentinel*, September 25, 1943.

12.Ibid.

13.Minutes of Powell Town Council meeting, November 5, 1943. Melvin Evans to Powell Town Council, November 5, 1943; Al Fryer to Powell Town Council, November 5, 1943, city records, Powell City Hall. *Powell Tribune*, December 9, 1943.

14.Minutes of Powell Town Council meeting, December 6, 1943.

15.*Heart Mountain Sentinel*, October 23, 1943.

16.Simpson, "Recollections of Heart Mountain," 181. Gwenn M. Jensen, "Illuminating the Shadows: Post-Traumatic Flashbacks from Heart Mountain and Other Camps," in *Remembering Heart Mountain*, 224.

17.*Powell Tribune*, November 4, 1943.

18.Minutes of Powell Town Council meeting, June 5, 1944.

19.Powell Town Council to Harold Ickes, June 5, 1944, Hunt Collection.

20.Powell Town Council to Lester Hunt, June 5, 1944, Hunt Collection.

21.Powell Town Council to Guy Robertson, June 5, 1944, Hunt Collection.

22.T. T. Dodson to Guy Robertson, June 14, 1944; Melvin Evans to Guy Robertson, June 16, 1944; Al Fryer to Guy Robertson, June 21, 1944, Hunt Collection.

23.*Powell Tribune*, June 29, 1944.

24.Al Fryer to Lester Hunt, June 21, 1944; Lester Hunt to Ora Bever, June 23, 1944, Hunt Collection.

25.Dillon Myer to Ora Bever, June 23, 1944, Hunt Collection. Minutes of Powell Town Council meeting, June 26, 1944.

26.Ora Bever to Lester Hunt, July 26, 1944, Hunt Collection.

27.Ibid.

28.Ibid.

29.Ibid.

30.Guy Robertson to Lester Hunt, July 27, 1944, Hunt Collection

31.Lester Hunt to Ora Bever, August 8, 1944; Ora Bever to Lester Hunt, August 12, 1944; Lester Hunt to Ora Bever, August 14, 1944, Hunt Collection.

32.William Bradley to Lester Hunt, August 22, 1944, Hunt Collection.

33.Lester Hunt to Ora Bever, August 31, 1944, Hunt Collection.

34.Guy Robertson to Lester Hunt, August 2, 1945; Dillon Myer to Lester Hunt, August 24, 1945, Hunt Collection.

35.Ibid.

Chapter 14

1.*Powell Tribune*, October 5, 1944.

2.Ibid.

3.*Personal Justice Denied*, 15.

4.Peter Irons, *Justice at War: The Story of Japanese American Internment Cases* (New York: Oxford University Press, 1983), 95, 255, 307-10.

5.Ibid., 319, 323-24, 343-45.

6.Guy Robertson, Memorandum to Dillon Myer, November 11, 1944, JAERP M1.09. *Powell Tribune*, December 7, 1944. *Heart Mountain Sentinel*, December 23, 1944.

7.Guy Robertson, weekly report to Dillon Myer, December 23, 1944, JAERP M1.09. Raymond Uno to author, May 2, 1993. A. T. Hansen, Community Analyst Trend Report, December 29, 1944, JAERP M2.37.

8.Ibid.

9.Ibid.

10.Ibid.

11.Ibid. Guy Robertson, weekly report to Dillon Myer, November 16, 1945, JAERP M1.10.

12.Guy Robertson, weekly report to Dillon Myer, January 13 and January 27, 1945, JAERP M1.10.

13.*Heart Mountain Sentinel*, February 24, 1945. Guy Robertson, weekly report to Dillon Myer, February 3, 1945, JAERP M1.10. Taylor, *Jewel of the Desert*, 217-18.

Notes

14. A. T. Hansen, Community Analyst Trend Report, February 9 and February 23, 1945, JAERP M2.39.

15. *Powell Tribune*, March 8, 1945. Glenn Hartman, Agricultural Section Final Report, February 15, 1945, JAERP M2.82.

16. Ibid.

17. Bill Hosokawa, "Different Kind of Vet," *Science*, January 1954, 24-25.

18. Ibid., 25-26.

19. *Powell Tribune*, March 8 and March 15, 1945.

20. *Session Laws of Wyoming*, 1945, Wyoming State Archives, Cheyenne, Wyoming.

21. Ibid. *Powell Tribune*, May 3, 1945.

22. A. T. Hansen, Community Analyst Trend Report, June 14, 1945, JAERP M2.39. *Powell Tribune*, June 14, 1945. Guy Robertson, weekly report to Dillon Myer, June 16, 1945, JAERP M1.10.

23. Dillon Myer to Lester Hunt, August 24, 1945, Hunt Collection.

24. *Heart Mountain Sentinel*, July 7, 1945. *Powell Tribune*, July 19, 1945. A. T. Hansen, Community Analyst Trend Report, July 13, 1945, JAERP M2.39.

25. *Heart Mountain Sentinel*, July 21, 1945. *Powell Tribune*, August 30, 1945.

26. *Heart Mountain Sentinel*, July 28, 1945. Guy Robertson, weekly reports to Dillon Myer, August 11 and August 18, 1945, JAERP M1.10.

27. Guy Robertson, weekly reports to Dillon Myer, August 25 and September 1, 1945, JAERP M1.10.

28. Guy Robertson, weekly report to Dillon Myer, November 16, 1945, JAERP M1.10. Ishigo, *Lone Heart Mountain*, 95-97.

29. Guy Robertson, weekly report to Dillon Myer, November 16, 1945, JAERP M1.10. *Powell Tribune*, November 1 and November 22, 1945.

Bibliography

Archival Sources

War Relocation Authority files cited were copied from the Japanese Evacuation and Resettlement Papers housed at the Bancroft Library, University of California, Berkeley. This collection is cited by report and reference number. Collections stored at the American Heritage Center, University of Wyoming, are cited by collection name only. All of the collections are listed in the finding aid under "Heart Mountain," therefore box and file numbers are not required when searching these collections.

The majority of internee recollections cited in this work are taken from letters written to the author. Former internees were asked a number of specific questions and asked to explain aspects of life at Heart Mountain which stood out most in their memories. These letters are in the author's possession.

Manuscript Collections

Federal Bureau of Investigation reports, Japanese Relocation Files, National Archives, Washington D. C.

Lester Hunt Collection, American Heritage Center, University of Wyoming.

Japanese Evacuation and Resettlement Papers, Bancroft Library, University of California, Berkeley.

John Nelson Collection, diary, TS, American Heritage Center, University of Wyoming.

Joseph C. O'Mahoney Collection, American Heritage Center, University of Wyoming.

Nels Smith Collection, American Heritage Center, University of Wyoming.

U. S. District Court for the District of Wyoming, National Archives-Rocky Mountain Region, Records of District Courts of the United States, Record Group 21, Denver, Colorado.

Minutes of Town Council Meetings, City Archives, Cody, Wyoming.

Minutes of Town Council Meetings, City Archives, Powell, Wyoming.

Bibliography

Unpublished Papers

Conley, Sam. "Forgiven But Not Forgotten," political science paper, TS, San Jose State University, San Jose, California, photocopy of transcript.

Hashimoto, Ruth. "Remembering With Gratitude," paper presented to University of New Mexico history seminar, Albuquerque, New Mexico, October 19, 1992, copy in author's possession.

Ito, Toshiko. "The Experience of One Second Generation American of Japanese Ancestry," paper presented to Laguna Hills United Methodist Church Women's Club, Laguna Hills, California, 1986, copy in author's possession.

Kondo, Kara. "Greatest Gift," copy in author's possession.

Tono, Jack. "The Trial and Tribulations of a Soldier for Righteousness," paper presented to Northeastern University of Illinois political science class, Chicago, Illinois, November 12, 1987.

Government Publications

Commission on Wartime Relocation and Internment of Civilians. *Personal Justice Denied*. Washington, D. C.: Government Printing Office, 1982.

Letters to Author

Araki, Bea. Letter to author, December 2, 1992.

Endo, Ada. Letter to author, November 30, 1992.

Eshita, Miyoko. Letter to author, May 2, 1993.

Hashimoto, Ruth. Letter to author, October 23, 1992.

Hashimoto, Ted. Letter to author, November 19, 1992.

Hatchimonji, Ike. Letter to author, October 27, 1992.

Hatchimonji, Mike. Letter to author, October 15, 1992.

Hayami, Frank. Letter to author, October 16, 1992.

Hori, Tatsu. Letter to author, March 1, 1993.

Bibliography

Hoshizaki, Takashi. Letter to author, November 2, 1992.

Hoshizaki, Takashi. Letter to author, June 9, 1995.

Hosokawa, Bill. Letter to author, September 22, 1992.

Hosozawa, Yoichi. Letter to author, November 15, 1992.

Igawa, Stanley. Letter to author, December 3, 1992.

Ikeda, Yasuko. Letter to author, October 26, 1992.

Inouye, Frank. Letter to author, October 15, 1994.

Inouye, Kaoru. Letter to author, November 16, 1992.

Ito, Toshiko. Letter to author, October 22, 1992.

Kinaga, Thomas. Letter to author, December 18, 1992.

Kondo, Kara. Letter to author, December 10, 1992.

Koshiyama, Mits. Letter to author, December 3, 1992.

Koshiyama, Mits. Letter to author, January 8, 1993.

Koshiyama, Mits. Letter to author, August 25, 1993.

Kuromiya, Emi. Letter to author, November 11, 1992.

Matsumura, Clarence. Letter to author, February 4, 1993.

Miyamoto, Connie. Letter to author, October 27, 1992.

Mori, Joyce. Letter to author, December 22, 1992.

Nitake, Toyoo. Letter to author, December 3, 1992.

Nozawa, George. Letter to author, April 16, 1995.

Ochi, May. Letter to author, October 30, 1992.

Oda, Jack. Letter to author, May 6, 1993.

Sakauye, Edward. Letter to author, February 19, 1993.

Sasano, Naomi. Letter to author, January 18, 1993.

Bibliography

Sasai, Eugene. Letter to author, March 7, 1993.

Shimada, Mori. Letter to author, February 5, 1993.

Sogioka, Yosh. Letter to author, December 5, 1992.

Tono, Jack. Letter to author, February 11, 1993.

Tono, Jack. Letter to author, April 19, 1993.

Tsuneishi, Arthur. Letter to author, November 13, 1992.

Uno, Raymond. Letter to author, May 2, 1993.

Ushijima, Jean. Letter to author, November 10, 1992.

Washizuka, Kohay. Letter to author, January 18, 1993.

Watanabe, Yoshio. Letter to author, November 12, 1992.

Yamashiro, Rose. Letter to author, September 19, 1992.

Interviews

Corbett, Clarissa. Interview with Patricia Hale, November 13, 1979, American Heritage Center, University of Wyoming.

Hosokawa, Bill. Interview with author, March 25, 1993, Laramie, Wyoming.

Ishi, Amy. Interview with Betty E. Mitson and Kristin Mitchell, July 9, and 20, 1973, California State University, Fullerton, Oral History Program, Wyoming State Archives, Cheyenne, Wyoming.

Kunitsugu, Katsumi. Interview with Sherry Turner, July 15, 1973, California State University, Fullerton, Oral History Program, Wyoming State Archives, Cheyenne, Wyoming.

Nishizu, Clarence. Interview with Richard Curtiss, January 1, 1966, California State University, Fullerton, Oral History Program, Wyoming State Archives, Cheyenne, Wyoming.

Okura, Ben. Interview with Bacon Sakatani, March 9, 1993, West Covina, California.

Okura, Frances. Interview with Bacon Sakatani, March 9, 1993, West Covina, California.

Bibliography

Sakatani, Bacon. Interview with author, March 30, 1993, Laramie, Wyoming.

Tono, Jack. Interview with Jean Brainard, May 13, 1992, Cheyenne, Wyoming, Wyoming State Archives.

Telephone Interviews

Fujishin, Sam. Interview with author, October 22, 1992 and August 31, 1993.

Honda, Harry. Interview with author, February 15, 1993.

Hori, Tatsu. Interview with author, January 10, 1993.

Matsumura, Clarence. Interview with author, November 10, 1992.

Sakatani, Bacon. Interview with author, July 28, 1993.

Newspapers

Billings Gazette (Montana)

Cody Enterprise

Heart Mountain Sentinel

Pacific Citizen

Powell Tribune

Rafu Shimpo

San Francisco Examiner

The Northern California Jewish Bulletin

Wyoming Eagle

Wyoming Labor Journal

Bibliography

Secondary Sources

Armor, John and Peter Wright. *Manzanar*. New York: Vintage Books, 1988.

Chuman, Frank. *The Bamboo People: Japanese-Americans Their History and the Law*. Chicago: Japanese American Research Project, 1981.

Conrat, Maisie and Richard. *Executive Order 9066: The Internment of 110,000 Japanese Americans*. Los Angeles: UCLA Asian American Studies Center, 1992.

Cray, Ed. *Chief Justice: A Biography of Earl Warren*. New York: Simon and Schuster, 1997.

Christensen, Paul. "An Evaluation of Certain Phases of Heart Mountain Elementary Schools." M. A. Thesis, University of Wyoming, 1943.

Daniels, Roger. *Asian America: Chinese and Japanese in the United States Since 1950*. Seattle: University of Washington Press, 1988.

____. *The Decision to Relocate Japanese Americans*. New York: J. B. Lippincott Company, 1975.

____. "Incarcerating Japanese Americans: An Atrocity Revisited." In Mackey ed., *Remembering Heart Mountain* and *Peace & Change: A Journal of Peace Research* 23 (April 1998).

____. *The Politics of Prejudice: The Anti-Japanese Movement in California and the Struggle for Japanese Exclusion*. Berkeley: University of California Press, 1962; 2d ed., 1972.

____. *Prisoners Without Trial: Japanese Americans in World War II*. New York: Hill and Wang, 1993.

Daniels, Roger, Sandra C. Taylor, and Harry H. L. Kitano, eds. *Japanese Americans: From Relocation to Redress*. Salt Lake City: University of Utah Press, 1986; revised, Seattle: University of Washington Press, 1991.

Drinnon, Richard. *Keeper of Concentration Camps: Dillon Myer and American Racism*. Berkeley: University of California Press, 1987.

Duveneck, Frank. "Evacuating American Citizens." *The Nation* (May 9, 1942).

Fischer, Louis. "West Coast Perspective." *The Nation* (March 7, 1942).

Fiset, Louis. "Health Care at the Central Utah (Topaz) Relocation Center." *Journal of the West* 38 (April 1999).

Bibliography

____. "The Heart Mountain Hospital Strike of June 24, 1943." In Mackey, ed., *Remembering Heart Mountain*.

____. *Imprisoned Apart: The World War II Correspondence of an Issei Couple*. Seattle: University of Washington Press, 1997.

____. "Thinning, Topping, and Loading: Japanese Americans and Beet Sugar in World War II." *Pacific Northwest Quarterly* 90 (Summer 1999).

Ganor, Solly. *Light One Candle: A Survivor's Tale from Lithuania to Jerusalem*. New York: Kodansha America, Inc., 1995.

Gesensway, Deborah, and Mindy Roseman. *Beyond Words: Images from America's Concentration Camps*. Ithaca: Cornell University Press, 1987.

Grodzins, Morton. *Americans Betrayed: Politics and the Japanese Evacuation*. Chicago: University of Chicago Press, 1949.

Hansen, Arthur. "The Evacuation and Resettlement Study at the Gila River Relocation Center." *Journal of the West* 38 (April 1999).

____. "Sergeant Ben Kuroki's Perilous "Home Mission": Contested Loyalty and Patriotism in the Japanese American Detention Centers." In Mackey, *Remembering Heart Mountain*.

____. "The 1944 Nisei Draft at Heart Mountain, Wyoming: Its Relationship to the Historical Representation of the World War II Japanese American Evacuation." *Magazine of History* 10 (Summer 1996).

Hansen, Asael. "My Two Years at Heart Mountain: The Difficult Role of an Applied Anthropologist." In Daniels, *Japanese Americans*.

Herzstein, Robert. *Henry R. Luce: A Political Portrait of the Man Who Created the American Century*. New York: Macmillan Publishing Company, 1994.

Hirabayashi, Lane. "The Impact of Incarceration on the Education of Nisei Schoolchildren." In Daniels, *Japanese Americans*.

Hohri, William. *Repairing America: An Account of the Movement for Japanese-American Redress*. Pullman: Washington State University Press, 1988.

Hosokawa, Bill. "Different Kind of Vet." *Science* (January 1954).

____. *Nisei: The Quiet Americans*. New York: William Morrow and Company, 1969; reprinted, Niwot: University Press of Colorado, 1992.

____. *Out of the Frying Pan: Reflections of a Japanese American*. Niwot: University Press of Colorado, 1998.

____. "The Sentinel Story." In Mackey, *Remembering Heart Mountain*, and *Peace & Change: A Journal of Peace Research* 23 (April 1998)

Ichioka, Yuji. *The Issei: The World of the First Generation Japanese Immigrants, 1885-1924*. New York: The Free Press, 1988.

____. *Views From Within: The Japanese American Evacuation and Resettlement Study*. Los Angeles: UCLA Asian American Studies Center, 1989.

Inglehart, Charles. "Citizens Behind Barbed Wire." *The Nation* (June 12, 1942).

Inouye, Frank. "Immediate Origins of the Heart Mountain Draft Resistance Movement." In Mackey, *Remembering Heart Mountain* and *Peace & Change: A Journal of Peace Research* 23 (April 1998).

Inouye, Mamoru. "Heart Mountain High School, 1942-1945." In Mackey, *Remembering Heart Mountain*, and abridged version in *Journal of the West* 38 (April 1999).

____. *The Heart Mountain Story*. Los Gatos, CA: Mamoru Inouye, 1997.

Irons, Peter. *Justice at War: The Story of the Japanese American Internment Cases*. New York: Oxford University Press, 1983; reprinted, Berkeley: University of California Press, 1993.

____, ed. *Justice Delayed: The Record of the Japanese American Internment Cases*. Middletown: Wesleyan University Press, 1989.

Ishigo, Estelle. *Lone Heart Mountain*. Santa Clara, CA: Communicart, 1972.

Jacoby, Harold. *Tule Lake: From Relocation to Segregation*. Grass Valley, CA: Comstock Bonanza Press, 1996.

James, Thomas. *Exile Within: The Schooling of Japanese Americans 1942-1945*. Cambridge: Harvard University Press, 1987.

Jensen, Gwenn. "Illuminating the Shadows: Post-Traumatic Flashbacks from Heart Mountain and Other Camps." In Mackey, *Remembering Heart Mountain*.

Kessel, Velma. *Behind Barbed Wire: Heart Mountain Relocation Camp*. Powell, WY: Published Privately, 1991.

____. "Remembering Heart Mountain Hospital." In Mackey, *Remembering Heart Mountain*.

Bibliography

Kessler, Lauren. *Stubborn Twig: Three Generations in the Life of a Japanese American Family*. New York: Random House, 1993.

Kikumura, Akemi. *Through Harsh Winters: The Life of a Japanese Immigrant Woman*. Novato, CA: Chandler and Sharp Publishers, Inc., 1981.

Larson, T. A. *History of Wyoming*. Lincoln: University of Nebraska Press, 1965; revised, 1978.

____. *Wyoming's War Years 1941-1945*. Palo Alto: Stanford University Press, 1954; reprinted, Cheyenne WY: Wyoming Historical Foundation, 1993.

Mackey, Mike. *Black Gold: Patterns in the Development of Wyoming's Oil Industry*. Powell, WY: Western History Publications, 1997.

____, ed. *The Equality State: Essays on Intolerance and Inequality in Wyoming*. Powell, WY: Western History Publications, 1999.

____. "Life In America's Concentration Camps." *Journal of the West* 38 (April 1999).

Mackey, Mike, and Steven Thulin. "Relocation of Japanese Americans During World War II: The Heart Mountain Experience." *Peace & Change: A Journal of Peace Research* 23 (April 1998).

____ , ed. *Remembering Heart Mountain: Essays on Japanese American Internment in Wyoming*. Powell, WY: Western History Publications, 1998.

Masaoka, Mike (with Bill Hosokawa). *They Call me Moses Masaoka*. New York: William Morrow, 1991.

McWilliams, Carey. "California and the Japanese." *The New Republic* (March 2, 1942).

Meyer, John. *Look Backs*. Long Prairie, MN: Neuman press, 1984.

Modell, John, ed. *The Kikuchi Diary: Chronicle from an American Concentration Camp*. Chicago: University of Illinois Press, 1973.

Myer, Dillon. *Uprooted Americans*. Tucson: University of Arizona Press, 1971.

Nakano, Mei. *Japanese American Woman: Three Generations 1890-1990*. Berkeley, CA: Mina Press Publishing, 1990.

Nakashima, Ted. "Concentration Camp: U. S. Style." *The New Republic* (June 15, 1942).

Nelson, Douglas. "Heart Mountain: The History of an American Concentration Camp." M. A. Thesis, University of Wyoming, 1970, (citations in this book are taken from Nelson's thesis and not his book).

Bibliography

____. *Heart Mountain: The Story of an American Concentration Camp*. Madison, WI: State Historical Society of Wisconsin, 1976.

Nuemann, William L. *America Encounters Japan: From Perry to MacArthur*. Baltimore: Johns Hopkins University Press, 1963.

Nobe, Lisa. "The Children's Village at Manzanar: The World War II Eviction and Detention of Japanese American Orphans." *Journal of the West* 38 (April 1999).

O'Brien, David, and Stephen S. Fugita. *The Japanese American Experience*. Bloomington: Indiana University Press, 1991.

Okada, John. *No-No Boy*. Seattle: University of Washington Press, 1976.

Okihiro, Gary. *Cane Fires: The Anti-Japanese Movement in Hawaii, 1865-1945*. Philadelphia: Temple University Press, 1991.

Okubo, Mine. *Citizen 13660*. Seattle: University of Washington Press, 1983.

Roberts, Philip. "Temporarily Side-Tracked by Emotionalism": Wyoming Residents Respond to Relocation." In Mackey, *Remembering Heart Mountain*.

Simpson, Peter. "Recollections of Heart Mountain." In Mackey, *Remembering Heart Mountain*.

Steidl, Franz. *Lost Battalions: Going For Broke in the Vosges Autumn 1944*. Novato, CA: Presidio Press, 1997.

Strout, Richard. "The War and Civil Liberties." *The New Republic* (March 16, 1942).

Takahashi, Jere. *Nisei/Sansei: Shifting Japanese American Identities and Politics*. Philadelphia: Temple University Press, 1997.

Takaki, Ronald. *Strangers from a Different Shore: A History of Asian Americans*. New York: Penguin Books, 1989.

Takezawa, Yasuko. *Breaking the Silence: Redress and Japanese American Ethnicity*. Ithaca: Cornell University Press, 1995.

Tateishi, John. *And Justice For All: An Oral History of the Japanese American Detention Camps*. New York: Random House, 1984; reprinted, Seattle: University of Washington Press, 1999.

Taylor, Sandra. *Jewel of the Desert: Japanese American Internment at Topaz*. Berkeley: University of California Press, 1993.

Bibliography

Thomas, Dorothy Swaine, and Richard Nishimoto. *The Spoilage*. Berkeley: University of California Press, 1946.

Van Nuys, Frank. "A Progressive Confronts the Race Question: Chester Rowell, the California Alien Land Act of 1913, and the Contradictions of Early Twentieth-Century Racial Thought." *California History* (Spring 1994).

____."Sowing the Seeds of Internment: James D. Phelan's Anti-Japanese Crusade, 1919-1920." In Mackey, *Remembering Heart Mountain*.

Weglyn, Michi. *Years of Infamy: The Untold Story of America's Concentration Camps*. New York: Morrow, Quill Paperbacks, 1976.

Index

Index